D0930634

# DISCOVERING
## THE HIDDEN WISDOM *of*
# The Little Prince

# DISCOVERING THE HIDDEN WISDOM *of*
# The Little Prince

## IN SEARCH OF
## SAINT-EXUPÉRY'S LOST CHILD

## PIERRE LASSUS

### TRANSLATED FROM THE FRENCH BY GRETCHEN SCHMID

Arcade Publishing • New York

First English-language Edition

Originally published in French by Éditions Albin Michel under the title *La sagesse du* Petit Prince: *À la recherché de l'enfant perdu avec Saint-Exupéry*

Arcade Publishing books may be purchased in bulk at special discounts for sales promotion, corporate gifts, fund-raising, or educational purposes. Special editions can also be created to specifications. For details, contact the Special Sales Department, Arcade Publishing, 307 West 36th Street, 11th Floor, New York, NY 10018 or arcade@skyhorsepublishing.com.

Arcade Publishing® is a registered trademark of Skyhorse Publishing, Inc.®, a Delaware corporation.

Visit our website at www.arcadepub.com.

10 9 8 7 6 5 4 3 2 1

Library of Congress Cataloging-in-Publication Data

Names: Lassus, Pierre, author. | Schmid, Gretchen, translator.
Title: Discovering the hidden wisdom of the Little prince : in search of
    Saint-Exupéry's lost child / Pierre Lassus ; translated from the French
    by Gretchen Schmid.
Other titles: Sagesse du Petit prince. English
Description: First English-language edition. | New York : Arcade Publishing,
    2017. | Includes bibliographical references.
Identifiers: LCCN 2017012325 (print) | LCCN 2017024094 (ebook) | ISBN
    9781628726848 (ebook) | ISBN 9781628726817 (hardback)
Subjects: LCSH: Saint-Exupéry, Antoine de, 1900–1944. | Authors,
    French—20th century—Biography. | Air pilots—France—Biography. |
    Saint-Exupéry, Antoine de, 1900–1944. Petit prince. | BISAC: LITERARY
    CRITICISM / Children's Literature. | LITERARY CRITICISM / European /
    French. | BIOGRAPHY & AUTOBIOGRAPHY / Literary.
Classification: LCC PQ2637.A274 (ebook) | LCC PQ2637.A274 Z74913 2017 (print)
    | DDC 843/.912—dc23
LC record available at https://lccn.loc.gov/2017012325

Cover design by Erin Seaward-Hiatt
Cover photo: Getty Images and iStock

Printed in the United States of America

*In memory of my grandfather, Henri Durand,*
*a hero of World War I*
*and the "pilots' barber" in Le Bourget from 1920 to 1950*

*"Unless you turn and become like children, you will never enter the kingdom of heaven."*
—Matthew 18:3


*"He needed to build his own footbridge over the abyss and rejoin the other part of himself, across space and time."*
—Antoine de Saint-Exupéry, *The Wisdom of the Sands*

# CONTENTS

DISCOVERING
THE HIDDEN WISDOM *of*
The Little Prince

# I

# THE END OF THE BEGINNING

JULY 31, 1944. BORGO military airfield, south of Bastia, Corsica, 8:00 in the morning.

The Lockheed P-38 Lightning F-5B N223, part of the II/33 Aerial Reconnaissance Group, First Squadron, is waiting on the runway. It has been selected for a mapping mission to prepare for the Allied landing in Provence that will take place in several days. The assignment is to photograph the Annecy-Chambéry-Grenoble region.

Lieutenant Duriez parks the jeep he has taken to collect the pilot from his quarters in Erbalunga, about fifteen kilometers away. He helps him put on his heavy, insulated flight suit and hoist himself into the cockpit. Perched on the wings of the aircraft, Sergeant Cotton and Airman Suty lend a hand as well, attaching the pilot's parachute and strapping him into his seat, putting on his helmet and oxygen mask, connecting the radio, and checking the instruments before closing the canopy. On the ground, Chief Warrant Officer Roussel and Chief Sergeant Potier check the engines, the landing gear, the flaps, the rudders, and the fuel levels. They remove the wheel chocks. The pilot makes the usual hand signal to indicate that everything is okay. He starts the engines, and the airplane begins to jolt along the runway before lifting off the ground.

It is 8:45. In the blue, cloudless sky, the Lightning's engines leave double contrails as the aircraft rapidly disappears into the horizon, toward French soil.

Lieutenant Commander Antoine de Saint-Exupéry has just taken off on his last mission.

GIVEN THE AMOUNT OF fuel on board, the flight can last between four and four and a half hours, so the aircraft should return around 12:15. At 13:00, the sky is still hopelessly empty, and anxiety levels on the ground are rising. Borgo's air traffic control, contacted one hour after the expected arrival, isn't able to offer any information. Three Vickers Warwick airplanes sent to search the sector bring back no news. Radar indicates that the Lightning hasn't crossed the French coast to return to the airbase. At 14:30, as the maximum flight duration has long since been exceeded, it is impossible that the aircraft is still in the air. In the evening, after verification that he hasn't landed at another Allied airstrip—which has happened before—Lieutenant Commander de Saint-Exupéry is pronounced "missing in action."

As with the Little Prince, who left to be reunited with his star, they will never find his body.

THE PILOT WHO HAS just disappeared was also a writer. He had published a number of works that brought him renown in France, England, Italy, and also the United States, where several of his books had been bestsellers. In 1939, *Wind, Sand and Stars* had received the National Book Award; that was the American title of *Terre des hommes*, which had received the Grand Prize for a Novel from the Académie Française that same year in France. In 1931, one of his earlier books, *Vol de nuit* (*Night Flight*), had been awarded the Prix Femina.

Antoine de Saint-Exupéry had been living since 1941 in the United States, where he had been miserable not to be part of the fight to liberate France. In the hope of rejoining the II/33 Aerial Reconnaissance Squadron with which he had served during the campaign to defend France in 1940, he managed with some difficulty to secure a berth on the SS *Stirling Castle*, which sailed on April 13, 1943, for North Africa, where American troops had landed the year before, on November 8, 1942. In his luggage, he brought a single copy of his latest book, which his New York editor, Curtice Hitchcock, had published for him in English- and French-language editions just one week before his departure. It was *The Little Prince*.

On this sunny early morning of July 1944, when Saint-Exupéry—after one last test of the engines—set off in his P-38 to conquer the French skies, he certainly could not have anticipated that his *Little Prince*, with over two hundred million copies sold in two hundred and seventy different translations, would bring him universal glory.

BY THE TIME HE secured his final mission, Saint-Exupéry may have sealed his own fate. Everything had seemed to oppose his taking command of the Lightning that day.

Already in 1939, after war was declared, he had had to fight hard and draw upon his fame and connections to be assigned to a combat unit, the II/33 Aerial Reconnaissance Group, based in Orconte in the Haute-Marne region of France. Most would have preferred that he work in the Information Services, directed by writer Jean Giraudoux, or at best as an instructor of aerial navigation—but certainly not as a fighter pilot. Moreover, at his medical checkup to be cleared to fly after he was called up in October, he was rejected for service: he had lived thirty-nine years, and his body bore the painful consequences of several of his previous accidents. But he couldn't stay on the sidelines, and he refused all the other postings that were proposed to him, despite everyone's attempts—including his close friends'—to convince him that he would be more useful alive than dead. For him, it was a question of honor: he didn't want to be taken for a coward, remaining in safety while his comrades were risking their lives. Such an attitude would have been "unchivalrous," as he told Léon Werth.[1]

Drawing on his numerous and powerful connections and making the authorities' heads "spin" with his incessant requests, he finally got what he wanted, or almost. Although he wasn't selected to pilot a fighter plane, he did join an aerial reconnaissance squadron on December 3, 1939, which was no less risky: only one in three missions returned to base. From March to June, he carried out seven missions, including one at very low altitude just above Arras on May 23. He brought back an aircraft riddled with bullets and a punctured oil tank. This flight would inspire him to write *Pilote de guerre*. Published in New York in February 1942 as *Flight to Arras*, the book would remain at the top of the bestseller list for six months.

In July 1940, Saint-Exupéry was demobilized and sent to Algiers, where the II/33 Squadron had taken refuge. One month before that, he had received a unit citation, the *Croix de guerre avec palme*.

He had done his duty.

When the Allies landed in Africa at the end of 1942, and France's liberation had been set in motion, Saint-Ex was living in New York, writing, delivering lectures, and—thanks to his public presence and his books—playing an influential role in improving the American public's perception of France. At forty-two years of age, after having fought courageously and risked his life doing so, it might seem that this sort of intellectual engagement should have been honorable and sufficient. So many would have been satisfied with that, and they said so, loudly and clearly. But not him. He wanted to rejoin his comrades, to be once again at the controls of an aircraft, to act, to push his commitment to the limits—and that implied facing death. This sense of moral obligation, which may have had to do with the "noblesse oblige" instilled in him by his aristocratic upbringing, was a part of his very being. Already in 1938, in an article published by the now-defunct French daily newspaper *Paris-Soir*, he had written, "Don't you understand that self-sacrifice, risk, loyalty unto death, these are behaviors that have contributed greatly to establishing man's nobility?"[2]

And yet no one wanted him to go. He was too old to pilot the new combat aircraft, which had evolved considerably since 1940; he was in poor health; he suffered from the sequelae of multiple accidents; and his morale was at its lowest point. His friends attempted to convince him that he would be more useful in the United States than in a war zone. His "woman friends" were sorry to see him go away, and feared for his life, while his spouse, the capricious Consuelo, was worried about maintaining her way of life on an officer's modest salary. As for the Gaullists, with whom he was in open conflict, they had no desire to see him return to a combat unit, since that would reinforce the prestige of General Giraud, who was then competing with de Gaulle to be the leader of Free France.

Once again, Saint-Exupéry called on his connections—both American, including General Doolittle, the commander of the Twelfth Air Force in North Africa, and French, including those closely connected with Giraud's advisors. His efforts paid off. In February of 1943, he was reinstated in the French army, and in April he was able to leave for Algiers.

In Laghouat, south of Algiers, he rejoined his comrades from the II/33 Aerial Group, which had become a part of the Allied air forces. He began to train again and obtained a certificate of aptitude for flying at high altitude, despite this note of caution: "Note that, while at a simulated low pressure corresponding to 39,000 feet, [experienced] mild pain at the site of an old fracture."[3]

On June 25, he was promoted to major and began training on a P-38 Lightning, with which the squadron had just been equipped. Only pilots under thirty were authorized to take command of this aircraft, which boasted state-of-the-art technology and remarkable performance but required perfect mastery of the controls. Once again, the forty-two-year-old Saint-Exupery obtained an exemption from the regulation; on July 21, over the course of five hours and fifty minutes, he undertook his first mission in a P-38, photographing southern France. His second mission, on August 1, went very badly: engine trouble forced him to turn around after forty minutes in the air. During the landing, he forgot to pressurize the hydraulic brakes, and the plane ended up in an olive grove, putting it permanently out of commission. The American commander, who had been jealously guarding his marvelous P-38s, was all the more furious that Saint-Ex had demonstrated a certain amateurishness during his training: on one occasion, he had flown at twenty-three thousand feet—instead of the sixty-five hundred called for—without an oxygen mask, because he had misinterpreted the navigational instruments. During another flight, he had opened the cockpit's vent window, as he was used to doing in the planes he had flown previously—but since the Lightning flew so much faster, the wind ripped his oxygen mask from his face. By the time he reached the ground he was woozy. In another training exercise, he had poorly prepared for landing and descended too quickly, causing damage to the aircraft's wings. The truth is that he had trouble with the plane's sophisticated instrumentation and hadn't taken enough time to completely master the machine.[4]

For some time, the Americans had been concerned about the pilot's idiosyncrasies, especially since his first mission over Provence, when he hadn't been able to resist the urge to photograph the château in Agay where his sister lived, a landmark of dubious strategic interest. The destruction of the P-38 after this latest mission was one incident too many. Saint-Ex was grounded. He made an attempt to seduce Colonel Dunn and Lieutenant Colonel Gray, the flight commander, by treating them to a Pantagruelian meal in an Algerian restaurant, in the hope they might reconsider. To better persuade them, he even spoke English, which was unusual for him: *I want to die for France.* . . . One of them replied with a categorical no, and the other responded that he may very well "die for France," if he felt so passionate about it, but not on board an American aircraft.

We know that, ultimately, this order wouldn't stand.

For nine months Saint-Ex moped, unable to take to the skies. He called on all his connections in order to be cleared to fly again. The goal proved extremely hard to achieve, for the Americans had no confidence in the pilot: he was too old, he was too tall for the Lightning's cockpit, he hadn't mastered the aircraft's one hundred and forty-eight instruments, he didn't speak English, he was absentminded, he suffered from both old and new wounds (he had recently injured himself by falling down the stairs), he was depressive, and he had a regrettable tendency to drink too much. As for the Gaullists, who were running the show now that Giraud was no longer in power, they had no desire to please a man who had refused to join them. Hadn't the General himself said to someone intervening on Saint-Ex's behalf, "Leave him in Algiers; he's only good for card tricks"?*

It was thanks to John Phillips, a *Life* magazine photographer, that Saint-Ex finally got what he wanted. In exchange for his writing several pages to accompany an upcoming photo essay, the magazine promised to pressure the authorities to restore Saint-Ex to his unit. Giraud also stepped in and made entreaties to General Dwight Eisenhower—none other than the commander in chief of the Allied Forces! Exasperated, Eisenhower reportedly declared, "This Saint-Exupéry is driving us crazy. Reinstate him! With any luck, he'll bother us less in the air than on the ground."[5] The provisional government's air commissioner, Fernand Grenier, finally "granted Major de Saint-Exupéry's request," and on May 16, 1944, Saint-Ex rejoined the II/33 group in Sardinia.

He received authorization for five missions. His flights were peppered with incidents, some more serious than others, and many of which were attributable to distraction or his whims. He would read detective novels while flying; he didn't

---

* Saint-Ex was an expert at card tricks, which he performed to entertain his friends.

understand instructions coming from the control towers, which were in English, and, by the same token, his messages to them were unintelligible; he repeatedly failed to deploy the landing gear until the last possible minute, which caused panic on the ground; he took off without realizing that one of the releasable fuel tanks hadn't been mounted to the aircraft, meaning that a single engine was forced to do all the work—and he didn't notice the problem until he had landed, when one of the propellers stopped turning on its own. Up until that moment, the wind flow had been making it spin.

His second mission, on June 6, was cut short by an engine fire. On June 14, his third mission was over Rodez. On the 15th, his fourth mission was ended by a problem with his oxygen mask. On the 23rd, on his fifth—and in principle, his last—authorized mission, he barely evaded a German fighter plane.

With the tacit permission of the squadron's commander, he carried out a sixth mission on the 29th, the day of his forty-fourth birthday. Engine trouble forced him to return at low altitude over Italy. Since the German air defense and fighter pilots couldn't believe an Allied plane might be flying overhead with such insouciance, Saint-Ex wasn't attacked, but he wasn't able to reach his base in Sardinia and landed instead in Corsica—in Borgo, where the II/33 group would relocate several days later. His seventh mission, over the Alps, was on July 11. On the 14th, his eighth was over Annecy. On the 18th, his ninth was over the Alps.

The squadron commander, Captain René Gavoille, consulted with General Chambe: they believed it was now imperative to keep Saint-Ex on the ground. High-altitude missions were exhausting for a man who freely described himself as "the most senior combat pilot in the world"[6] and who was in poor health besides. They formed a plan to brief him about the Allied landing in Provence scheduled for mid-August, which would entail a mandatory grounding, since it was unthinkable that a pilot possessed of such vital information might be shot down and made prisoner by the enemy. But they dragged their feet, and Saint-Ex obtained a tenth mission on July 31.

On the evening of the 30th, he left his quarters and went out to eat with several new friends, in the village of Miomo, near Bastia, in a little restaurant right on the beach. He was quite cheerful, performing card tricks and telling funny stories.[7] He left relatively early, around 23:30. What did he do next? No one knows, but he hadn't returned to his room by 1:30. Noting his absence, the operations officer, Jean Leleu, started to worry, as pilots scheduled for a mission were supposed to go to bed early the night before. He designated Captain Siegler as Saint-Ex's replacement.

Early on the morning of the 31st, while Siegler was having breakfast and prepping for his flight with Lieutenant Duriez, Saint-Ex suddenly appeared in the mess hall. Spotting Siegler, he realized he'd been replaced and became angry. Under his furious gaze, Siegler made no objection and left. Saint-Ex climbed into Lieutenant Duriez's jeep, which took him to the field where the P-38 Lightning F-5B N223 awaited him.

For fifty-four years, no one knew what had become of the pilot and his aircraft. Every possible hypothesis was proposed, including the most fanciful, until in October 1998 a fisherman from Marseille, Jean-Claude Bianco, recovered the pilot's silver identification bracelet in his nets from the waters of a rocky inlet on the Mediterranean coast. Subsequent searches in the vicinity led to a diver named Luc Vanrell discovering the wreckage of the Lightning on May 24, 2000, nine hundred twenty feet below the surface, not too far from the island of Riou. Among the pieces were an undercarriage, a portion of the cabin, and a turbo-compressor. They were brought to the surface at the end of 2003, and experts attested that they were indeed part of the plane that Saint-Ex had flown on July 31, 1944. They were then presented to the Air and Space Museum in Le Bourget, a commune just northeast of Paris.

But one mystery remains: how did Saint-Ex end up under the sea? The belated statement issued in 2008 by a German pilot named Horst Rippert, claiming that he had shot down the Lightning, isn't credible. No German aviation report at the time recorded the kill, and Rippert is known to be a mythomaniac; it's also difficult to believe such a person would have kept silent for sixty-four years!

And so? Victim of German antiaircraft fire? Pilot error? Lack of oxygen? Technical malfunction? . . . Or suicide?

Though this last hypothesis might seem implausible, given that Saint-Ex was scrupulous about completing every mission, it cannot be set aside entirely. The man was depressed and, it seems, didn't relish confronting the world as he imagined it was becoming. On the evening before his death, July 30, he had written to his friend Nelly de Vogüé, "I've almost died four times. I feel staggeringly indifferent about it." Earlier, he had written her, "And besides, I've had enough of myself . . . . I'm discouraged, discouraged." And again: "My morale? Oh, it's not great. I cannot bear these times, I cannot. Everything has gotten worse. It's dark in my head and cold in my heart. Everything is mediocre. Everything is ugly."[8] To his friend, Doctor Georges Pélissier, he had written in June of 1943, "Old friend, I can't take it anymore tonight. It's sad—I wish I liked life just a little, but I barely like it at all. When I thought the other day that I was done for, mid-flight, I wasn't sorry about it." His last letter, which was addressed to Pierre Dalloz and was found on his table after his disappearance along with the July 30 letter addressed to Nelly, ended thus:"If I am shot down, I will regret absolutely nothing. The termite mound of the future terrifies me, and I hate the robotic righteousness of men. I myself was made to be a gardener."These are moving, but troubling, statements, put in writing just hours before his last flight.

Equally troubling is the eyewitness account of a German officer, Erick Herot, who reported that on July 31, 1944, he saw an Allied plane skimming the surface of the sea near Marseille before crashing under the waves.[9] This account seems not to have been taken into consideration previously because, at the time, it was thought Saint-Ex had disappeared near Nice or Menton. But if this were true, it would invalidate the theory that his death was linked to an attack by a German plane, or fire from an antiaircraft gun.

From this brief recap of the events that marked Saint-Ex's career as a military pilot, it can be observed that, beginning with his induction in 1939, obtained only "as a favor," up until the morning of July 31, when another pilot was chosen to carry out the mission, all the gods seemed to have joined forces to prevent him from taking off that morning. But faced with each obstacle, he rebelled, refusing to follow the path that destiny seemed to have traced for him. He had his own way, and he pursued it: "The individual is only a path,"[10] as he put it in *Flight to Arras*. He used his cunning, skirted obstacles, took evasive action, and dodged and skirted difficulties in order to accomplish a different destiny than the one assigned him—in order to be faithful to his future, as though he had a rendezvous that he had to keep at all costs. But with whom?

At the time of his disappearance, Saint-Ex had just published his last book, *The Little Prince*, which came out on April 6, 1943, seven days before his departure for Algeria. Four works had preceded it: *Southern Mail* in 1929, *Night Flight* in 1931, *Wind, Sand and Stars* in 1939, and *Flight to Arras* in 1942.[11] One book, *The Wisdom of the Sands*, or *Citadelle* ("citadel") in French, would be published posthumously in 1948. The first four were directly inspired by his experience as a pilot. In a certain sense, they have an element of journalism, even though their literary quality elevates them to something much more prestigious. *The Wisdom of the Sands*, on the other hand, with its two hundred nineteen chapters, is a longer work than all of the others combined, and can be considered a sort of "philosophical chant" that lends itself to three different readings: legendary, cultural, and spiritual, taking on a Biblical tonality. It was the "great work," *the* book on which he toiled for years—since 1936, it seems. He never parted with its innumerable pages, which he labored over with extreme attention to detail, revising them endlessly. The author never completed it, although the work was eventually published.

And so, among all of Saint-Ex's writings—between the works published while he was alive, comprised of brief narratives about events that directly concerned the author, and his posthumous work, which resembles a poetic or philosophical chant, or perhaps a moral testament—we find one that seems completely different, a dreamlike story presented as a "tale for children," a work in which the author's text and illustrations are inextricable: *The Little Prince*.

Another of this book's peculiarities: Saint-Exupéry apparently took great pleasure in writing it, which seems to have been fairly unusual for him. It is all the more unusual given that at the time, during his American exile, he was in a bad state psychologically, socially, and domestically. His biographer, Stacy de La Bruyère, writes that Silvia Hamilton-Reinhardt, a friend of Saint-Ex's at whose place in New York he would frequently spend time to write, reported that "she often heard him chuckle with pleasure while writing his story."[12] By setting aside the text's obvious charm and poetry and analyzing it "coldly," from a distance, it can be observed that all of the themes and even the characters of *The Little Prince* can be found scattered, here and there, throughout Saint-Exupéry's earlier writings. It is as though Saint-Ex, deliberately and consciously—or perhaps not—brought together in this little story the essential part of the message that he had wanted to deliver through the rest of his opus: as though this tale explains the very essence of the author, and condensed his substance.

And what if *The Little Prince* were a culmination?

What if, when he was ensconced in Silvia Hamilton-Reinhardt's living room to write and draw, he "chuckled with pleasure" because he had finally found himself again, because he was finally overcoming his exile—his self-exile—because he was finally reunited with his "beginnings," his childhood? "And so, I seem to have come to the end of a long pilgrimage. I have discovered nothing, but as though waking from sleep, I simply see again what I was no longer looking at," he wrote in *Flight to Arras*.[13] And what if the "teachings" of *The Little Prince* were to be found here: in this reunion, this rediscovery of a childhood that everyone vaguely yearns for, to put their scattered days back together again and experience their life's meaning, to become who they truly are?

# 2

# A STRANGE LITTLE STORY

ONCE UPON A TIME, there was an aviator who succeeded in landing his broken-down plane in the desert. There can be no doubt that he must have been a very good pilot, for he managed to touch down amid the sand dunes without major damage.

Unfortunately, he found himself a thousand miles from any human habitation, and all alone. At the time, airplanes were very rudimentary flying machines that couldn't radio for help. Since he couldn't expect to survive more than eight days on his reserves of water, he had to find a way to repair his aircraft by himself: it was a matter of life or death.

As night had already fallen, he had gone to sleep on the sand, when he was awakened by a funny little voice asking him to draw a sheep. It was the voice of a funny little man who didn't look at all like a child lost in the desert a thousand miles from any human habitation. And this little man, who was quite solemn and completely out of the ordinary, merely repeated his request without responding to the stunned aviator's questions about what he was doing there: "Please . . . draw me a sheep . . ."

That's how it began.

The aviator and the little man stay together for eight days, alone in the middle of the desert. We learn quickly from the

pilot—for he is the one narrating the story—that the funny little man is a little prince. We don't know what type of prince he
is, for there are in fact many different kinds of princes, from the
Prince of Darkness to prince consorts. In any case, it is somewhat doubtful that he's the son of a king, because he never
mentions his father, or his mother either, for that matter. Maybe
the aviator has given him this title because the child is dressed
like a prince: with a very long green cloak with red lining that
falls to his feet, beautiful boots that go up to his knees, gold
stars on his shoulders and, in his left hand, a sword—maybe a
saber.

At least, that's how he looks in the portrait that the aviator
made of him later on, stipulating that, while this sketch is the
best he could manage, nonetheless it is "far less ravishing than its
model." Here, it's important to clarify that, in order to tell us the
story of this extraordinary adventure, the aviator isn't satisfied
with merely writing it down. He illustrates his tale with drawings, many drawings—forty-six at our count, in just eighty-six
short pages—the style of which is certainly a little childish but
all the same quite well done. This is all the more surprising,
given that he began the story by telling us that, at the age of six,
he had been discouraged by adults from pursuing a career as a
painter. In fact, in his first drawing, these same adults had seen
only a hat, whereas the child had actually drawn a boa constrictor digesting an elephant. And so, when the little prince made
the odd request that he draw a sheep, the aviator responded that
he didn't know how to draw, other than the outside of boa constrictors digesting elephants, or else the interior of boa constrictors, allowing you to see the pachyderm within. It is therefore
remarkable—surprising, even—that this encounter with the little prince allowed our storyteller to give himself permission to

draw, despite the very discouraging verdicts of the grownups to whom he'd shown his sketches up until now.

That said, we should point out that the little man appears dressed as a little prince only once. Subsequently, he's depicted as a simple little boy, clothed in a sort of green tunic with a belt and wearing shoes—or perhaps slippers would be more apt—that are dark colored. Nothing princely in all that. The only remarkable features are his hairstyle, which is thick and curly and gold in color, and a very long scarf, also gold and usually floating behind him as though blown up by a violent wind. It almost looks like a banner, or—since the artist is an aviator—the contrail that airplanes leave behind them in the sky; or might it even replace the wings that the little prince had before, which allowed him to fly? He wears a red bow tie only once, while perched on his very small planet, contemplating the stars. (We forgot to mention that, before his arrival on Earth, this little prince lived all alone on a small asteroid.) We see him without his scarf only twice more: when lying in the grass and crying after having realized that the flower that bloomed on his planet is only an ordinary rose and when, having been bitten by a yellow snake, "he fell softly, as a tree falls."

From all this, we can conclude that the outfit is not what makes him a little prince.

Perhaps he owes this princely quality to the fact that he rules over his planet (which, just between us, isn't all that surprising, given that he lives there by himself)—the B-612 asteroid, an object scarcely bigger than a house. As he tries to repair his machine, the aviator learns from the little prince that he "lived on a planet that was hardly bigger than himself" and that he had left it, no doubt taking advantage of a migrating flock of wild birds, because he was leading "a melancholy little life" and needed a friend. And so, to learn about them and find an occupation, the little prince visited other asteroids closest to his home, six in total, before coming to Earth.

Over the course of the narrative, we learn about the little prince, his little planet where baobabs and flowers grow and volcanoes burn without erupting, and we learn that during his travels he met some eccentric characters—oddly, only men—as well as flowers and animals. When he arrived on Earth, he worried about not finding many people about—of course, he *was* in the middle of a desert—and the first living thing with which he exchanged any words was a snake, the "color of the moon." Next, he found roses, a lot of roses: five thousand in a single garden! Let's add that he was devastated by this, for he realized that his own flower, the only one on his planet and with which he'd had a complicated relationship, was nothing but a simple rose. He wept . . . but later on he was consoled a bit by his very fruitful conversation with a fox, who taught him many things. By taming the fox, he made a friend of him. He then met a railway switchman who directed trains full of people in a hurry first to the right, then to the left. He also made the acquaintance of a vendor selling pills that allowed people to save time, because if they swallowed one pill a week they would no longer need to drink water. In short, some very odd men.

Finally, he met the aviator.

It's this aviator who tells us the story, and he relates very few of the little prince's own words: the little prince speaks only 265 times—we counted. That isn't a lot for an entire book. Let's add that, when he does speak, the little prince is very sober in tone: ninety-two of those times he only asks a question, 158 times what he says requires only one sentence, and eighteen times it's just a single word. So we can only hope that in recounting the little prince's peregrinations the aviator is faithfully recalling what he heard.

They live side-by-side for a week. While the aviator tries to fix his plane, he listens to the little prince, he questions him and responds to his questions, even when he doesn't really want to because he's worried about the repairs he has to complete. But the little man never gives up on a question once he's asked it. The aviator draws sketches for him: the sheep, of course, and the box the sheep comes in—but unlike the grown-ups, who couldn't see the elephant inside the serpent, the little prince can see the sheep inside the box perfectly well—and also a muzzle so the sheep won't eat the one, very precious flower that grows on the little planet. Because the little prince called his attention to the dangers baobabs pose for the planet, the aviator creates a magnificent sketch—he says himself that it's the handsomest of all his drawings—in which we see these trees devouring a poor asteroid with their giant roots. He does this as a warning to children not to let baobabs grow just anywhere.

At the end of the week, when they come close to dying of thirst, the little prince and the aviator discover a well. The airplane is now repaired, the aviator will be able to leave the desert, and the little prince announces that he must return to his planet that very evening with the help of the snake—surely, the same one he encountered when he arrived on Earth, who told him that he'd be able to "take him farther than any ship." It is the anniversary of the little prince's arrival on Earth, his star is right above the spot where he landed a year ago. It's for that reason that he has returned to this precise place, exactly where the aviator was with his broken-down plane. Yet the little prince's star is too far away for him to take his body with him, for it is much too heavy. Accordingly, he has asked the snake—whose venom is very effective—to bite him and free him from the envelope of flesh that's so hard to transport. He's sad to leave the aviator, especially since the aviator will believe him to be dead, though that isn't actually the case. Although the little prince asked him not to do so, the aviator goes with him and sees the snake bite him. The little prince doesn't cry out; instead, he falls gently, without a sound because of the sand.

The aviator is finally consoled when he realizes that the little prince isn't dead and that he was able to return to his planet. The proof is that when the sun rises the next morning, he isn't able to find the little prince's body. From then on, he listens to the stars at night, and he hears them laugh because the little prince, just as he had promised, is laughing on one of them, and it's as if all of the stars are laughing for the pilot. His only worry is that he forgot to add a leather strap to the muzzle so the little prince can attach it to the sheep, and he wonders what might have happened on the little planet: did the sheep eat the flower?

IT IS THUS A strange little story that Antoine de Saint-Exupéry tells us, and quite different from what he wrote in his other books. Those are completely "serious" books, that relate his adventures as a pilot and address subjects like war, peace, relationships among men, and the world's joys and sorrows: other ways to conduct ourselves in our lives, in our relationships with other humans and with nature. At first glance, by contrast, *The Little Prince* resembles a fairy tale, a tale for children. Saint-Exupéry asks forgiveness for not dedicating it to children but rather to an adult, his friend Léon Werth—because he, as a Jew and a member of the Resistance in German-occupied France, has to go into hiding and "needs a lot cheering up." He is careful all the same to amend this dedication: "To Léon Werth when he was a little boy," because, after all, "all grown-ups were children first (although few of them remember it)."

One has to wonder what impelled the writer-pilot to write a tale, especially during a very difficult time for the world—it was wartime—and for himself in particular. He was in exile in America, far from his friends and family and more or less rejected by compatriots, who reproached him for not clearly aligning himself with the Free French forces, and he still hadn't fully recovered from injuries suffered during a bad plane crash in Guatemala.

Some propose that it was during his hospitalization in Los Angeles, where he was being treated for his injuries, that the idea for the story came about. Annabella, a Hollywood actress whose real name was Suzanne Georgette Charpentier and who was married to the famous actor Tyrone Power, visited Saint-Ex frequently in his hospital room. She had played the leading role in the movie *Anne-Marie*, directed by Raymond Bernard in 1935, for which he had written the screenplay. To keep him company, Annabella read him Hans Christian Andersen's *Fairy Tales*, and one of them, "The Little Mermaid," may have inspired Saint-Ex to create a fairy tale for children himself. According to another variant, it was his American editors, Eugene Reynal and Curtice Hitchcock, who asked him to write a Christmas story. They weren't very pleased with the result, however: the little prince's "death" at the end seemed inappropriate for a Christmas story, but Saint-Exupéry stubbornly refused to change his work. It's also said that Eugene Reynal's wife, Élizabeth, who was moved by Saint-Exupery's deep moral anguish during the dark year of 1942, suggested that he invent a story for children as a form of therapy using the little men he was in the habit of drawing almost obsessively, in letters, in the pages of books, and on napkins in restaurants. But it could be that Saint-Exupéry himself had wanted for a long time to write a fairy tale. It could be that he'd proposed a story of this sort to an editor many years earlier. There's a suggestion of this in an article published in the newspaper *Paris-Soir* on May 14, 1935. While leaving for Moscow on a reporting assignment, Saint-Ex found himself on a night train seated across from a couple whose child had fallen asleep. The writer was filled with wonder at the grace of this little child, whom he thought had a "musician's face." He saw him as a "child Mozart" and wrote, "Little princes in legends were no different from him. . . ." This is the first evocation of a little prince in Saint-Exupéry's writings, and it seems even more significant in that, wondering about the child's future, he compared the care that would have to be lavished on him in order for him to grow to what gardeners have to shower on a "new rose" that is born by being relocated in a garden: "You must isolate the rose, tend to the rose, give it special care. . . ."[1] As early as 1935, almost ten years before publishing his most famous work, Saint-Exupéry was already associating a little prince with a rose! And during the same period, when he found himself in Moscow one day, he asked a diplomat to draw him a sheep: a strange premonition.[2]

No matter what set in motion the writing of the book, the result can be considered an "unidentifiable piece of literature," at least compared to the author's other works. *The Little Prince* is unique because of its very form, but also because of what would become of it. Certainly, Saint-Exupéry's works were all successes in the world of publishing, printed by the hundreds of thousands and translated into numerous languages; but those successes, which many authors would envy, don't compare to

*ce*, a true publishing phenomenon that would
he Bible, the Quran, and *Quotations from Chair-*
*ng*, the most-read book in the world.

consider that level of popularity a publishing

reasons for it are complex, diverse, and differ-
er. Still, for the book to "speak" to millions of
ountry, every culture, and to all ages, it must be
*Little Prince* resonates with fundamental and
d emotions. The German theologian Eugen
afraid to call it "a true breviary of hope, the
."3

ination of its literary virtues and the author's
be that this tale—purportedly more philo-
dren—bears a universal humanist message
r can recognize him or herself not only
onate with a "rational" code of ethics but
sion of a collective unconscious?

BEING," is omnipresent in the book. Not
prince, its hero, but it begins with the
 six years old . . ." and ends by evoking
child comes to you . . . be kind! Don't
me quickly to say he has returned."
Note also that the aviator makes a point of telling us that he's
beginning his narrative six years after the departure of the little
prince, as though the story were a return to its own infancy.

Throughout the text, the "grown-ups"—unlike the children—appear as odd, bizarre, rather stupid, and devoid of any
poetry: "They always need explanations"; "Grown-ups never
understand anything by themselves"; "Grown-ups are truly

very strange," etc. It follows that the child is the one Saint-Exupéry entrusts to convey a message addressed to all mankind, as though this child were its keeper, as though he alone could understand and express it—as though the child were the very essence of being human.

But the ability to see a child as a master of wisdom isn't universally shared, to say the least. Why does Saint-Exupéry have it? Why is he possessed of such nostalgia for a lost childhood that he struggles to keep alive nonetheless, as if it fulfilled a vital need? He found peace only by discovering the little prince, a child who was in reality a recreation of himself as a child: "And so I lived alone, without anyone I could truly talk to, until my plane broke down in the Sahara desert six years ago." Sentences from an earlier draft that were not retained in the final text are perhaps even more revealing: "As I'm rather on the sidelines, I never told the grown-ups that I wasn't like them. I hid from them the fact that I've always been five or six years old at heart."[4]

Might *The Little Prince* be the palimpsest of Saint-Exupéry's childhood? And what in particular from his childhood could explain the author's ability to deliver such a universally understood message, regardless of its essential meaning? Does its universality stem from the fact that it is a child who gives it voice—a child who, unlike the grown-ups, knows the truth of the world and is a master of wisdom, just as certain spiritual traditions teach? Might the child be the true forebear to the man, one forgotten or lost in transit and whom grown-ups needed to find within themselves in order to know harmony, to accede to their own truth? Let's note in passing that such a depiction of the child appears in a foundational text, the Gospel, as the Christian-educated Saint-Exupéry would certainly have known. Matthew the Evangelist tells us, "At that time Jesus declared, 'I thank thee, Father, Lord of heaven and earth, that thou hast hidden these things from the wise and understanding and revealed them to babes'" (Matthew 11:25).

So how, and to what extent, did the author's childhood inspire and nurture this tale? Might we draw from it any lessons about what a child needs in order to become a grown-up at peace with the world, with others, and with him- or herself, capable of a *compassionate* humanity?

# 3

# AN ENIGMA ALL THE SAME?

"A MAINSTAY OF FRENCH literature."[1] One of only two texts (along with Kafka's *The Castle*) that are "essential and characteristic of our centuries of bloody and devastating conflict." "The ideal character, humanity's dream."[2] "We don't need to mourn the Brothers Grimm when fairy tales like *The Little Prince* can still emerge from books about aviators and those who follow the stars."[3] *Giving Existence Meaning or Why* The Little Prince *Is the Greatest Metaphysical Treatise of the 20th Century.*[4] It's impossible to tally the number of gushing reviews and expressions of hyperbolic praise coming as much from prominent figures as from anonymous readers on Internet forums: "This book is a true masterpiece, halfway between a tale for children and a lesson for life!"; "A book that will never die, intended for readers of all ages, attesting to the richness of childhood, and in a more general sense, of life. The reflections in this fabulous adventure uplift the reader, leading him straight to what is essential." Or another: "A book that can't be overlooked! I read it and reread it to my children when they were little. You have to read and meditate on each short passage in order to understand the full richness of this book 'for children.' For me, it's a major work of philosophy that invites us to draw closer to others in order to understand and love them, and especially to take our time, to set aside time for ourselves and for others."

It may be surprising to learn that *The Little Prince* is said to have been the favorite book of the philosopher Martin Heidegger, who supposedly annotated every page of his personal copy. But it was also the favorite of James Dean; the statue at the site of the accident that cost Dean his life bears the inscription, "What is essential is invisible to the eye," which is probably the most famous quotation from the book. Yet it's hard to discern what—besides a passion for *The Little Prince*—the German philosopher, now controversial for his links with Nazism, and the role model for rebellious teenagers could possibly have in common. What is the "genius" of this text that allows it to bring together individuals who are otherwise so disparate?

There are certainly critics of the book, such as these anonymous ones in forums: "The problem with *The Little Prince* is where to situate it. If it's a book for children (eight or nine years old, no older), then let's call it nice. If it's a book for adults, then it's very poorly written and very, very silly. In any case, it is the most overrated book in all of literature." Or another: "When people claim this is a very profound work, I have to wonder why. After rereading certain passages, I don't wonder anymore. In fact, if it's a book for adults, then it's superficial and badly written, and if it's a book for kids, then it's acceptable, except for the simple fact that they'd prefer to read the Countess of Ségur, *Treasure Island*, Jules Verne & Company . . . although I do really like the watercolor illustrations."

We should note that these criticisms are largely in the minority. As such, we would be justified in considering them negligible, strictly speaking—all the more so because the book's extraordinary popularity has definitively tipped the balance in favor of praise. However, they can be useful as a way to encourage us to take a step back and pose a simple question, or at least simple in its formulation: what message, what teachings, does *The Little Prince* contain?

INTERPRETERS OF THE TEXT most often point to several phrases with a strong ethical charge as expressing the essential message of what would ultimately be a philosophical tale. The most commonly quoted ones are: "One can see well only with the heart. What is essential is invisible to the eye"; "Only children know what they're looking for"; "Grown-ups never understand anything all by themselves"; "People don't have the time anymore to learn anything"; "People don't have any imagination. They repeat whatever they're told"; "Language is the source of misunderstandings"; "I should have judged based on her actions and not on her words"; "It's lonely among men too"; "You become forever responsible for whatever you've tamed," etc. If we could take away only one lesson, without a doubt it would have to be the idea of a "hidden truth" inaccessible to grown-ups, who, unlike children, worry only about material things, trivialities, or cold, hard cash, and who speak in a language that is by its very nature deceitful. Thus, the truth is found in actions and not in words, an idea reminiscent of Simone Weil and the action theorists. To this should be added the idea of a general sense of responsibility toward others, or in any case toward those one has "tamed," which evokes the philosopher Emmanuel Levinas.

The enigma of *The Little Prince*, then, would reside in the fact that its extraordinary popularity is associated with a fairly banal philosophical, humanist, and ethical message. Even regarding it simply as a fairy tale for children—which it should have been, according to the editors' initial request—the narrative would hardly seem thrilling to the mind of a child drawn to extraordinary adventures, twists and turns, fear, joy, excitement, suspense, and, fundamentally, opportunities to identify with heroes who triumph over terrifying dangers, escape cruel fates, or vanquish invincible enemies. Nor does the tale—since that's how it's characterized—refer to universal archetypes linked to a collective subconscious filled with elemental fantasies that organize the human psyche and arise from the confrontation with parental imagos (such as the fears of devoration, engulfment, and so on, etc.). In short, Jim Hawkins of *Treasure Island* or Harry Potter are more relatable and more exciting heroes for children than a little prince from a miniscule planet in conversation with a businessman, an alcoholic, and a lamplighter. "Little Red Riding Hood" or "Hop-o'-My-Thumb' ("Little Poucet") address primitive fears more directly and more powerfully than a child who has fallen from the sky, with no family or friends other than a tenuous relationship with a capricious rose, who faces no threat other than the risk of an outbreak of anarchic baobab trees.

The most famous and "fundamental" fairy tales, if we limit our focus to them, feature formidable characters who directly threaten one or more children, and most often these persecutors are the parents themselves, or at least adults who play some sort of parental role: parents who abandon their children in the forest so they'll die of hunger ("Hop-O'-My-Thumb"), a father who wants to rape his daughter ("Donkeyskin"), a mother who deliberately exposes her daughter to mortal danger ("Little Red Riding Hood"), a stepmother who abuses her stepdaughter ("Cinderella"), another who tries to kill her ("Snow White") . . . there is no lack of examples. However, in

*The Little Prince*, there aren't any villains, only characters who are ridiculous (the king or the vain man), pitiable (the alcoholic or the lamplighter), obsessive (the businessman or the geographer), or stuck performing silly tasks (the railway switchman or the pill merchant). None of them is frightening or worthy of hate—nor of love either, other than the rose and the fox, once it's tamed.

Can the little prince himself really be viewed as a fairy-tale character? Many have thought Saint-Ex was inspired by Andersen's "The Little Mermaid," while others have compared his little prince to the heroes of "Fanchon, the Cricket,"[5] "Little Pierre,"[6] *The Little Princess,*[7] *Peter Pan,* and even *Tintin.*[8] But this line of thinking doesn't offer much promise. In his notes on the French version of the text, Michel Autrand writes of the little prince, "His childish appearance was not important. It's much more about man, and specifically the man Saint-Exupéry—past his fortieth birthday, in wartime, prone to gravest of doubts—searching for meaning in his life."[9] Saint-Ex is recounting his story more than spinning a tale. The narrative speaks much more about the "real" than it does about the "fantastic," apart from the little prince's wanderings among the stars. The desert and a pilot with a malfunctioning plane come directly from an adventure that Saint-Ex lived. The sheep are the ones he saw every day in Africa. The fox is virtually identical to the fennec fox that he tamed. He feared snakebite when he stayed with the Fuchs family in Argentina and the charming daughters teased him, saying there were snakes under the table, as he relates in *Wind, Sand and Stars.* When he worked for the Tuileries de Boiron tile factory or selling Saurer trucks, he encountered many a businessman and geographer obsessed with numbers. He crossed paths with plenty of drinkers when he frequented the cafés at

Saint-Germain-des-Près. The baobabs of Senegal, the volcanoes of the Amazon, wells in the desert, the stars that allowed him to navigate during his night flights: all the "material" of the story was drawn from his own memories, even the little prince himself, whom he had already been drawing on any fragment of paper within reach—a little character who strangely (or not) resembles the young Antoine himself, with blond, curly hair that can be seen in his childhood photos.

So, if *The Little Prince* isn't a fantastic tale but more a metaphor of the author's life, and if it's neither a philosophical dissertation nor a moral treatise, what explains its universal success?

# 4

# A PLANET HARDLY BIGGER

# THAN A HOUSE

It's a shame that the Saint-Exupéry family didn't have the equivalent of a Jean Héroard, the doctor assigned to the dauphin who would one day rule under the name of Louis XIII. Thanks to him, we know everything about the future monarch's childhood, day after day, for Héroard recorded even the least of his actions. But when setting out in search of the little prince in his creator's childhood, one quickly finds oneself empty-handed. The Saint-Exupéry children were surrounded by governesses—or more precisely, *Fräuleins*, for they were all German until 1914—but none of them left any journals, nor did anyone else in the family's entourage. Antoine himself scarcely referred to his childhood, at least not in any direct way, even if it left traces throughout his oeuvre. Until he began his studies at Lyon at a Christian Brothers school, there is barely anything from which to recreate his first years other than scattered confidences, a mention here or there in his writings, remarks collected from his mother, Marie, and the memories that his sister Simone recorded in her short book, *Five Children in a Park*. Very little, in truth, and the same anecdotes are sprinkled throughout the many biographies—mostly remarks about his Aunt Tricaud's château, with its innumerable and mysterious nooks, its linden trees, its park, the animals the children played with, its housekeepers and manservant. The biographies also inevitably narrate young Antoine's "displays of virtuosity," including the invention of a flying bicycle that never actually took off at all and his tinkering with a small gas engine that ended up exploding, slightly injuring his little brother François. In actuality, there was nothing very exciting. Stories of taming a little white rat and of the death of a bird nourished with bread soaked in wine take on an epic quality, evoking the novels of the Countess of Ségur.

It's a shame that we don't have more concrete, personal, and precise information about this essential period of Saint-Ex's life, from birth to the age of ten. The lessons of clinical psychology have shown how the earliest interactions, in the first months and years, between a child and his familial and social environments play a crucial role in forming the child's character. The family's history, what we know of the social practices of the time and in this very particular milieu of French nobility, the accounts of his mother (who died in 1972, almost a centenarian) and his sisters Simone and Gabrielle, and what he himself set down in writing, all give us an idea—although only a very general one—of Antoine's early childhood. We know only the broad outlines of what happened and can even evoke an ambiance, a certain aura, but more than anything we're aware of the silences.

Antoine Marie Jean-Baptiste Roger de Saint-Exupéry was born on June 29, 1900, in Lyon to Jean Martin Louis Marie Marc de Saint-Exupéry and Marie Louise Andrée Boyer de Fonscolombe. His paternal grandmother was born Alix Bouquier de Trélan and his maternal grandmother Alice de

Romanet de Lestrange. Although he never made much of it, his aristocratic origins would obviously have a defining influence on his personality. Two girls had been born before him: Marie-Madeleine, or "Biche," in 1897, and Simone, or "Monot," in 1898. His brother François was born in 1902 and his sister Gabrielle, or "Didi," in 1903. The parents, Jean and Marie, were distantly related. They had met at the house of the Countess of Tricaud, born Gabrielle de Lestrange, godmother and great-aunt of Marie. Gabrielle de Tricaud, who was a widow and who had lost her only daughter, was very attached to her god-daughter and played matchmaker, presenting her with a partner who was her equal in rank. The marriage took place on June 8, 1896.

But their family life suffered a catastrophe on March 14, 1904. Just as Marie and Jean arrived at the château in the commune of La Môle, which was the property of Marie's parents, Jean collapsed in a small train station in La Foux in the Var department of southeastern France after suffering a stroke. Despite the intervention of a doctor who was at the scene, he died in his wife's arms. Marie found herself a widow at the age of twenty-eight, without any source of income and with five children to support. It was her godmother, the Countess de Tricaud, who would take charge of the little tribe, letting them stay in her large apartment in Lyon during the winter and in her château in Saint-Maurice-de-Rémens the rest of the year. This property, which included a vast park with plenty of pine and linden trees, was *the* childhood home of Saint-Exupéry. It is this house, simultaneously familiar and mysterious, that he would evoke numerous times when remembering his childhood days: the games with his sisters and his brother, the time of insouciance, love, and security.

Marie de Saint-Exupéry was a warm, indulgent, and protective mother. The daughter and granddaughter of composers, she herself was an excellent musician, and all the children received a musical education. She also painted, wrote poetry, and carried on an abundant correspondence. Although she was raised in a very traditional environment, she wasn't lacking in imagination, and even had certain iconoclastic tendencies: in a short story, for example, she wrote of her childhood disappointment in noting that two "princes," the Duc de Chartres and the Comte de Paris, who had come to dine at her parents' house, weren't anything out of the ordinary, and that she'd even been tempted to stick her tongue out at them. In addition to his passion for drawing, Antoine inherited his mother's diffidence toward— even defiance of—conventions. She was also very pious and nothing shook her faith, not even the periods of bitter mourning: her husband brutally gone from the world just as she had given birth to their fifth child, her son François dead at the age of fifteen, her daughter Marie-Madeleine dead at thirty, and finally Antoine, who disappeared in 1944 and whom she would survive by twenty-eight years.

But returning to the château's park and its maze of rooms: the sisters and brothers were living out their childhoods according to their different personalities. They built tree houses, put on plays, played a lot of music, and invented wonderful games, like the Chevalier Aklin game, which consisted of running outside during a thunderstorm while trying to avoid the raindrops. Each one chose his or her own passions: gardening, botany, breeding various animals, writing, and already for Antoine, inventing, with his plans for the flying bicycle. The eldest, Marie-Madeleine, nicknamed "Biche," was fairly shy, reserved, and solitary. She was passionate about animals and plants, which she painted in her sketchbooks. The second, Simone, nicknamed "Monot," was rather unruly, capricious, and undisciplined. She, too, drew and made up stories, which she would illustrate in her journals. Then came Antoine, or "Tonio," the first son, who was also nicknamed the Sun King because of his crown of blond curls—which reminds us of another character. His sister Simone said he had "a little factory in his brain, endlessly producing new ideas. As soon as the harvest was gathered, it fermented and germinated. He would draw inferences, develop theories, construct machines."[1] He was boisterous, aggressive, rather undisciplined, and fairly tyrannical, especially toward his younger brother whom he tried, without great success, to order around as he pleased. Antoine was passionate about reading and about the stories that his mother would tell him as he followed her from room to room, dragging his little chair after him in order to sit close to her and listen to her in conditions of optimal comfort. Very early on, he began to write short poems, which he would force his family to listen to, at all hours of the day and night (as he would continue to do for the rest of his life); he would even fight his little brother if he refused to listen. His brother François, nicknamed the "Gros Père" (literally "fat father"), was a calm, meditative child, gifted in his studies and in music, who possessed a sometimes mordant sense of humor. He may have admired his older brother's energy and creativity, but he knew how to defend himself against his brother's attempts at domination. The two brothers argued and fought often, to the great despair of Aunt Tricaud, who much preferred the girls, who were markedly less unruly. Finally, the little one, Gabrielle, nicknamed Didi, who would remain Antoine's favorite sister, was possessed of a strong character—methodical, obstinate, and dominating. She knew how to get what she wanted through spectacular displays of emotion: torrents of tears or soul-splitting wails, which greatly impressed the entire family circle. According to Simone, it was she who inspired Antoine's characterization of the child Geneviève in *Southern Mail*: "You were so well protected by this house, and by the living garment of earth that surrounds it. You had made so many pacts with the linden trees, the oaks, and the herds, that we voted you their princess."[2]

Following a brief spell at a Christian Brothers school in Lyons, in 1909 Antoine and his brother were enrolled in the Jesuit school of Notre-Dame-de-Sainte-Croix in Le Mans, the same school his father had attended. Marie split her time between Lyons, where the girls remained, and Le Mans. In her absence, it was Fernand, the boys' paternal grandfather, who watched over them. The school was harsh and the distance proved to be too great, so in 1915 Antoine and François moved to a school run by the Marianist order in Fribourg, Switzerland, at the Villa Saint-Jean. This was closer to Lyons and to Saint-Maurice-de-Rémens, and they appeared to take much better to its pedagogy, which was inspired by the British education system. In 1912, claiming he had permission from his mother—a bald-faced lie—Antoine received his air baptism on the little airfield at Ambérieu, near Saint-Maurice, where he had gone to admire the first very rudimentary airplanes. The first crossing of the Channel in an airplane, by a pilot named Louis Blériot, had taken place just three years earlier, in 1909. The pilot Gabriel Wroblewski-Salvez, moved by the boy's passionate interest and convinced that his mother, who had accompanied him several times to look at the amazing machines, had given her permission, settled Antoine into a Berthaud-Wroblewski and took him around the airfield twice.[3] The seeds of his vocation were thus planted. The experience was not completely without risk: some time later, the same airplane would crash, killing the pilots and the engine's inventors, Gabriel and Pierre Wroblewski.

After World War I, which affected the Saint-Exupéry family just as deeply as it did all the families in France, a new tragedy struck them directly on July 10, 1917. François, who had been suffering from rheumatic fever—untreatable at the time—passed away at the age of fifteen. He was in the company of his brother at Saint-Maurice. Antoine would rarely reference this grief, but he wrote it into a very moving passage of *Flight to Arras*. He had been called to his brother's bedside when the end seemed near, and his brother, just minutes before passing on, told him: "I wanted to speak to you before dying. I am going to die," and he bequeathed to him a toy steam engine, a bicycle, and a rifle. Saint-Ex ended the passage in *Flight to Arras* in this way: "My brother told me, 'Don't forget to write about all of this. . . .' When one parts with one's body, the essence is revealed. Man is nothing but a tangle of relationships. Those relationships are the only things that matter. The body, that old thing, is left behind."[4] Later, the little prince would say, "You understand, it's too far. I can't carry this body! It's too heavy."

Perhaps this is when Saint-Exupéry's childhood ended. Up until then, his life (outside of boarding school) had been marked by the children's great closeness to one another and to their mother within a very well-protected environment. Their very attentive and very indulgent mother reassured and consoled them. She was, and would stay, irreproachably loyal to all of her children. Even when Antoine became famous, she refused to let the others be overlooked: "Antoine was gifted, of course, but all of my children were gifted. I can't say that I noticed, at that time, that Antoine was more so than the others."[5] She was their savior, and it was to her they turned when they were confronted with life's sometimes-painful realities. To Antoine, she would always represent a beneficent divinity, the ultimate fallback, as this letter, among dozens of others he wrote to her in 1922, proves: "If you knew how, every day, I learn to love you a little more. . . . I need you as much now as I did when I was little. . . . You are what is best in my life. . . . It is true that you are the only consolation when we are sad. When I was a kid, I would return with my heavy knapsack on my back, sobbing because I had been punished, you remember, in Le Mans . . . and by simply hugging me, you would make me forget it all. You were an all-powerful source of support against our supervisors and prefects. We felt safe in your house, we were safe in your house, we belonged only to you, and all was well. Well, now it's the same thing: you are the refuge, the one who knows everything, who can make us forget it all, and, whether we want to or not, feel like little children again."[6] Marie's tendency to indulge her children did not go uncriticized by the paternal side of the family, who predicted that the boys would become utterly useless. So, when at twenty-nine Antoine was named the operations manager of the Aeroposta Argentina company in Buenos Aires, he thanked his mother for having resisted the family's stultifying pressures thus allowing him to fulfill his potential: "It's a nice vindication of your child-rearing, don't you think? You were reproached for it so much. It's not bad to be the director of such a large outfit at twenty-nine, is it?"[7]

Within the little clan, they were well-protected under the benevolent authority of their mother, who respected her children's personalities, and of their aunt, the Countess de Tricaud, who may have been somewhat strict but was also generous and affectionate. Saint-Ex's childhood and adolescence took place in an atmosphere of security and calm, despite some economic difficulties and, of course, the war, which disrupted their lives. But we must add nuance to this idyllic portrait by noting that the children grew up in an environment almost entirely devoid of men. François's very premature death signaled the end of their carefree days. Their father had died in 1904, their Aunt Tricaud had long since been widowed, their maternal grandfather, Charles de Fonscolombe, had died in 1908, and their paternal uncle and Antoine's godfather, Roger de Saint-Exupéry, who had been the closest to the children, was killed in the first days of the war in 1914. Their paternal grandfather, Fernand de Saint-Exupéry, who was quite old, lived in Le Mans and had only occasional contact with his grandchildren up until his death in 1918. In Saint-Maurice-de-Rémens, the only men were Henri, the coachman and faithful valet (but unfortunately also an alcoholic); Cyprien Lutzelschwab, a Swiss citizen, whom they dubbed "Zizi the Toad"; the family doctor, Joannès Rendu; the Colonel de Saint-Didier; several old bachelors who played bridge with their aunt; an old foreign mission priest who regaled the children with tales of his life in Africa; and the inevitable parish priest, Father Montessuy.

The absence of a masculine, paternal role model in a young boy's family circle cannot have been without consequence in the shaping of his identity. This is all the more true in that, in the society of the time, the place and the role of the head of the family—a close descendent of the Roman concept of the all-powerful *Pater familias*—had an importance that was symbolic as much as it was social and legal, and was much more pronounced than it is today. Antoine, bolstered as he was by the unconditional support of his mother, viewed the supposed authority of the masters he encountered during his boarding-school years with a sense of casualness. He would always be inclined to exempt himself from established rules and to bypass hierarchies, finding in his mother an indulgent and available ally who would always gladly call upon her relations to obtain special privileges for him.

Without a doubt, his lack of a father during childhood and adolescence helps explain his complex relationships, which ranged from rejection to requests for recognition, with other representatives of masculinity. During his life, he cultivated particularly strong and loyal friendships with assertive men who possessed knowledge, power, competence, or moral qualities that gave them legitimate authority with regards to Saint-Ex's own values, from Jean Mermoz to Henri Guillaumet, Léon Werth, and of course Didier Daurat, the famed operations director of Latécoère who later become the unyielding head of Aéropostale. Daurat was the inspiration for the character of Rivière in Saint-Exupéry's second novel, *Night Flight*, and its true hero, as well as the one to whom it was dedicated.

But this entourage consisting exclusively of a mother, sisters, aunts, and governesses might also shed light on the absence of female characters in *The Little Prince*. If we maintain that the writer's process of conceiving of the fairy tale and bringing it to life included a quest to bridge a gap between himself and his childhood, we can understand why women, who were superabundant in the writer's real world, might have disappeared in his imaginary one. They weren't the ones missing from his life, either when he was a child or when he was in New York beginning the draft of his book. As General de Gaulle would say during a press conference about his successor, "What should be feared is not the void but the excess."

This points us toward the silences that—like the dark matter that remains undetected but nonetheless represents more than five times the universe's detectable matter—appear to be largely predominant in Saint-Exupéry's childhood.

In the family history, there was a major rupture, a tragedy that was foundational in the sense that the future lives of the mother and her children would be completely shaken by it: the father's brutal death, which was completely unforeseeable and very premature. It plunged the family into disarray—social and economic, of course, as overnight Marie was deprived of income and had to take charge of five young children at a time when social aid didn't exist—but also emotional. They had probably suffered a cataclysmic affective disarray. And yet there was practically never any discussion about this part of the family drama. Their economic difficulties were scarcely mentioned, though, of course, those were relative, for their generous Aunt Tricaud took charge of the family and ensured that they had very adequate living conditions. Upon her death, in 1920, she bequeathed her property to Marie, providing her with a modest, but sufficient, income. But more questionable was the silence about the emotional and psychological consequences of this cruel grief. Saint-Ex himself would never speak of it directly. His sister Simone, in *Five Children in a Park*, would make short work of the question in five lines: "The five children are orphans. Their father, Jean de Saint-Exupéry, who was full of happiness after the birth of his fifth child, Gabrielle, has died at forty-one years of age. What will become of the young widow, stricken with grief? She will pull herself together before the task at hand: raising five children. Alone? No, Aunt Tricaud is there."[8] The funereal tribute is brief, and the emotion is, to say the least, contained. Yet, at the time of her father's death, Simone was six and her elder sister Marie-Madeleine seven—ages at which a child is conscious of death. We don't know under what the conditions the tragedy was announced to the children, and a fortiori, how they reacted. But there can be no doubt they witnessed the pain of their mother, their grandparents, and the rest of their family, and that they perceived their mother's helplessness when faced with the responsibilities that she, a young woman, had to take on alone. No matter how the adults acted—no matter how strong their emotional control and their ability to hide their suffering and anguish from the children—it is well known that emotion is unconsciously "porous" between people who are close, and it would have been impossible for the children, even the smallest ones (four-year-old Antoine, two-year-old François, and three-month-old Gabrielle) not to have been profoundly affected to the core of their personalities, which were beginning to take shape.

So, what was the reason for this powerful, sustained silence? Was it the family's values in an environment of "noblesse oblige," in which it wasn't appropriate to show one's emotions (although Marie de Saint-Exupéry, who expressed herself through music, painting, and poetry, wasn't closed off to feeling)? Was it the desire to act correctly and the belief, however erroneous, that by not speaking about it, the children would be protected from sadness? Or, perhaps, was it some secret about this brutal death? We don't know. But, today at least, it is well established that the unsaid—keeping silent—offers no protection at all; to the contrary, it feeds fantasies and fosters pathogenic "crypts," hidden graves of trauma that are passed down from generation to generation. Antoine would never write or speak of his father, but his memory would haunt him in hypochondriacal fantasies. As Stacy de La Bruyère explains, "He thought his father had died of syphilis, and that this disease was hereditary. It wasn't a preposterous idea at a time where the disease was responsible for 15 percent of the general mortality rate, but all the same, it was a particularly insidious worry for a young man with a prodigious imagination."[9] We'll return to this later.

But maybe we should turn to *The Little Prince* to search for this forbidden mourning—for the trace of this lost and apparently forgotten father, the father of whom nothing remained, not even words, not even grief.

According to the most common hypothesis, Saint-Exupéry wrote the tale in response to a demand from his New York editor, Curtice Hitchcock (or from his other editor's wife, Elizabeth Reynal), to bring to life the little man he drew almost obsessively on any piece of paper within reach. This meant there would be a child who speaks in the story. Children who speak are in tales everywhere, from the fairy tale *Hop-o'-My-Thumb* to *Alice in Wonderland* to *Peter Pan*. Saint-Ex's child would be a prince—a little one, but certainly a prince—which is to say that he would belong to an elite, descended from a prestigious lineage, a member of the nobility. After the death of his father and his grandfather, Antoine himself inherited the title of "count," even if he didn't publicly claim it. The little prince has "golden hair," which is a curious coincidence: describing her younger brother as a small child, Simone de Saint-Exupéry wrote, "His blond, curly hair made a brilliant halo. We called him the Sun King."[10] This little prince with blond hair was therefore literally produced by one who was called a "king," thus conforming to the rules for the transmission of noble titles. What this demonstrates is that the little prince character is a representation—and a fairly close one—of Saint-Ex as a child.

Moreover, this little prince "fell from the sky," almost as the aviator with his broken-down plane "came" from the sky, a very similar concept. However—and this is an important difference—the little prince comes from "another planet." He takes his time in responding to the precise questions of the pilot, who wants more detail: "It took me a long time to understand where he came from. The little prince, who asked me so many questions, never seemed to hear my own. It was only thanks to words uttered by chance that, little by little, all was revealed to me."[11] The child is reluctant to explain where he comes from, and it is no doubt not by chance that he reveals himself only through words spoken "by chance." But in the end, we finally do learn that "his own planet was hardly bigger than a house," a comparison that brings to mind Saint-Exupéry's childhood home—more precisely, the château at Saint-Maurice-de-Rémens, which he evokes numerous times in his writings and which, in the tale's narrative, is evoked in the first allusion the aviator makes to his childhood. He speaks of the house when, threatened by the prospect of dying of thirst, he goes in search of a spring*: "When I was a small boy, I lived in a very old house, and according to legend, a treasure was buried there. . . . My house was hiding a secret deep in its heart."[12] Simone de Saint-Exupéry recounted that the children searched for treasure with "gold necklaces and diamond jewelry," but in the attic they found only "trunks stuffed full, some made of studded wood, others of black leather trimmed with yellow"; however, "how moving it was to discover in one of them

---

* The French word here, *source*, means both "spring" and "source"—referring to one's roots or origins—and better expresses the author's dual meaning. "Spring," unfortunately, doesn't have quite the same connotation.

an assortment of canvas suits with sophisticated waistcoats, my father's wardrobe. . . . "[13] These traces of their father, buried in a trunk in the depths of the attic—couldn't this be something of a treasure?

But unlike Antoine's childhood castle, the little planet that the extraordinary little man comes from is quite desolate. The little prince lived a "melancholy little life" there. We can understand why. He was alone, with no human or animal presence— only a few plants, including the baobab sprouts he had to watch for constantly and some "very simple flowers, with just one row of petals." There was also one newcomer: a rose, certainly very beautiful and moving—it was the least she could be, after having taken such care with her appearance—but so capricious that she drove the little prince to leave. In addition, there were two active volcanoes, very useful "for warming up one's breakfast in the morning" and not dangerous because they were regularly and carefully cleaned. All this is well and good, but we can understand how he might have grown bored. And so, the little prince left to discover the vast world, no doubt to escape the rose's whims but also because he "needed a friend." On the B-612 asteroid, his only distraction was the "pleasure of the sunsets"; and even though by "dragging his chair several steps" he could see forty-four in just one day, we can well imagine that the spectacle would eventually become tiresome. Besides, the little prince explains that these sunsets are especially beautiful "when one is so sad"—and here we are: here is someone who isn't happy. But isn't this a bit perplexing? If one can see forty-four sunsets (and thus as many twilights), then one should also be able to contemplate forty-four sunrises. Poets and psychiatrists alike will tell you that sunrises have much a more positive and stimulating effect on the psyches of spectators. Could our little prince be taking pleasure in melancholy? The fact is that in order to watch the sunsets, the little prince has to "pull his chair," which logically must also be small—just like young Tonio's, whose mother reported, "He followed me like a shadow everywhere in the house with his little lacquered chair, so that he could sit next to me wherever I was."[14] Despite this analogy, though, it's doubtful that the real Saint-Exupéry's childhood was bathed in the same twilight atmosphere as the little prince's planet.

Ultimately, the B-612 asteroid seems unwelcoming, not exactly a place one can imagine living out one's days—so it's surprising to learn that the little prince wants to return there after his journey. Why did Saint-Exupéry make his little prince live on this miniscule, inhospitable planet, lost in the middle of "millions and millions of stars"?

The answer can be found in what we've already understood: that, in imagining this tale, Saint-Exupéry split himself. On one hand, he is the aviator with a broken-down plane in the desert, as had happened to him; and on the other hand, he is the child with golden curls that he once was, pulling his little chair behind him. But while his aviator self remains faithful to the reality of his life—right up to his fear of dying of thirst—Tonio never lived in a desolate universe. His privileged childhood realm of Saint-Maurice-de-Rémens was, as we have seen, a kind of mini paradise. So why this little barren planet, rotating tirelessly in the sidereal void and in silence? This little planet swept by "drafts" of wind, where at night "it was very cold," is a bit like the moon, that night star that waxes, wanes, disappears, and is reborn: a star that follows the laws of birth and death, associated in Hebrew mythology with the rebellious and independent Lilith, who was Adam's first wife, before Eve.

Something of Saturn, too, "gloomy and taciturn, and presid[ing] over the affairs of time," as the French singer and poet Georges Brassens sang, with its repetitive sunsets. We can understand the child's reluctance to say exactly where he comes from: an empty house, full of drafts, and perhaps concealing "a secret deep in its heart"—perhaps a weighty secret.

As we know nothing about the little prince's origins, neither where or from whom he was born, he appears to have been created from the same substance as the asteroid—unless, like the rose, he "came from a seed." Saint-Exupéry brings "his" child to life again in an unlikely and cold place, unconnected to the rest of the universe, and so a mystery weighs on the question of what enabled him to come to his little world. In the beginning, the aviator doesn't know where the child comes from. He learns only "by chance, in course of reflections," and when he finally knows that he comes from the B-612 asteroid, his curiosity is only very partially satisfied. But in wanting, whether consciously or not, to arrange a meeting or—even better—a reunion between himself and the child that he was, Saint-Ex couldn't limit himself to drawing on the happy memories of his carefree days at Saint-Maurice. This is because he knew that child well—the one who ran in the park, made motors explode, and invented revolutionary processes for watering the garden. He never left that child, and he thought about him often—so he's not the one Saint-Ex needed to find again. It's the "before" that he was curious about, because he wasn't born all of a sudden under a linden tree in the park or in the hallways of the château that he transformed into a land of adventures with his brothers and sisters. He needed to reassure himself that he was truly himself—the one and only—and to go all the way back to the beginning: from whom was he born? And it seems that he didn't have much to go on in order to imagine this original world: some trinkets, some ordinary flowers, and little volcanoes that don't amount to anything at all. Even those few things were learned only in fragments and by chance, in the course of reflections—probably those of grown-ups overheard in a dark hallway, where stern uncles talked among themselves after dinner without realizing that a child was hiding in a shadowy corner.[15] So, all that remains is a little planet, where the life hidden underground reveals itself only in the heat and smoke of the volcanoes that spit out fumes into the sky from their depths. As a result, he goes to find the adult that he has become, so the adult can draw him life in order to animate and invigorate his deserted, wildly spinning little star. And that life takes the form of a sheep.

# 5

# FROM ONE STAR TO THE NEXT

IN SEPTEMBER OF 1917, several weeks after his brother's death, Saint-Exupéry arrived in Paris to enroll as a boarder at the École Bossuet and take preparatory classes at the Lycée Saint-Louis in order to prepare for the entrance exams for the École Navale, the French naval academy. In October 1926, Didier Daurat, the operations director of the Latécoère aircraft company, hired him on trial as a pilot for the Toulouse-Dakar mail line. After passing the required courses to learn how to repair the engines, Saint-Ex flew his first mail run in the springtime, sitting alone at the controls of a Breguet 14.

Between the moment when he left his little planet for the capital and October 19, 1927, when he would be named the airfield chief of Cap Juby in Morocco—a refueling and maintenance stop for aircraft between Agadir and Saint-Louis in Senegal—ten years of wandering, new acquaintances, training, love, friendship, discovering independence, and discovering life had occurred. Like the little prince, in order "to find an occupation and to learn," Saint-Ex had visited other asteroids, met various characters, discovered many places, and picked up all sorts of knowledge, all things that were quite foreign to the familiar and comfortable life he had led up until then. Antoine was searching for himself: what and who would he become? Which career, which way of life, which commitments would he choose; what would be the answers to fate's endless questions? What was he seeking and what did he desire? Was he the little Sun King, Tonio, whimsical, inventive, and rebellious? Was he Antoine, passionate, shy, and loyal? Was he the Count de Saint-Exupéry, a member of high society, sometimes frivolous but ready to give up his life for a question of honor, "noblesse oblige"? Certainly, he was all of these, one after the other and all at once, with returns and advances, flashes of one and avoidances of another. In short, they were ten years of messy confrontations with the realities of a world that was opening its unfamiliar horizons to him and alternately beckoning, resisting, wounding, or threatening the identity of a young man seeking a way to unite the scattered truths inside him.

Among the planets he visited, there were certain obligatory stops, including high school and the Bossuet dormitory where he lived while preparing for his École Navale entrance exams. The naval academy was a funny idea for someone who was rather more literary than mathematical, not to mention: the sea? Certainly, there had been several marine officers in his lineage, and for an aristocrat, the Royal Naval Division remained prestigious. But Saint-Ex would not know glory on that planet. He was more of a dilettante when it came to his studies. He met new friends and went out into the world surrounded by close relatives—female, mostly, among them the seductive Yvonne de Lestrange, with whom he was more or less in love. He became familiar with Paris and its accompanying lifestyle. He played practical jokes and seemed already interested in "*mignonnes*" or "easy girls," not to say prostitutes. During this period the war dragged on, and Paris was directly threatened by the Ludendorff offensive of 1918. Antoine and his friends would climb onto the roofs to watch Big Bertha's bombardments and the murderous ballet of the Gothas* overhead, until, faced with the danger of the approaching German troops, the school was moved south of Paris, to Sceaux. In short, there were many distractions, the details of which Saint-Ex's mother followed closely; she worried for her son, but was always generous and indulgent, providing him with an ample allowance.

Naturally, he failed at the École Navale and fell back on fine arts and architecture as an auditor—and a very casual auditor at that. He drew a lot, as we've already seen; since very early on, the letters he sent to his mother, sisters, and friends were illustrated with drawings, often captioned cartoons representing the characters or knick-knacks he was surrounded by. But more than that was needed to become an architect, and at any rate, he held no illusions about his talent. "My drawings are just awful,"[1] he would complain in a letter to his mother, and "I don't know how to draw. . . . Darn!"[2] Later he would sketch portraits, often of women, that showed real talent.[3] It seems he spent much more time sitting in sidewalk cafés than in front of his easel at the École des Beaux-Arts.[4] He made the acquaintance of the painter Bernard Lamotte, whom he would encounter again in New York during the war; it was Lamotte who would illustrate *Flight to Arras* and at one point be approached to illustrate *The Little Prince*. Lamotte didn't take Saint-Ex's vague aspirations

---

* Big Bertha was a long-range howitzer artillery gun installed in the Saint-Gobain forest in Aisne, which bombed Paris, taking many victims. The Gothas were German biplane bombers responsible for nearly a thousand victims in Paris.

seriously. "It really must be said: Saint-Ex was as much of an architect as I was a dentist. He himself must have wondered sometimes what he was doing at Beaux-Arts. His passion for architecture wasn't exactly all-consuming. If you crossed the Rue Bonaparte around noon and went into the Jarras bistro on the corner, you would find him there, seated at a table, scribbling on a piece of paper. He was clearly a writer, determined to become famous."[5]

In reality, young Antoine professed no such ambition: "What I will become ten years from now is the least of my worries."[6] However, he did have curious fantasies from time to time, almost premonitions, about his future: "When I'm an engineer and a writer, when I have plenty of money, when I have three cars, we'll travel to Constantinople together."[7]

Evidently this planet with its serious inhabitants wasn't made for him. There must have been too many kings and vain people.

DURING THE SAME PERIOD, he visited a satellite planet much more assiduously, a more attractive one by far: the planet inhabited by his family and societal relations, by friends from high society. They were people who lived in the townhouses, on Rue Saint-Guillaume or Rue de La Chaise in the very aristocratic 7th arrondissement of Paris: Henry de Ségogne, Bertrand de Saussine (who was the brother of Renée, nicknamed Rinette, with whom he would fall in love), Albert de Dompierre, Élie de Vassoigne, and Louise de Vilmorin. Among his close Parisian friends who opened their doors to him were his aunts, Alix and Anaïs de Saint-Exupéry, who brought him to dine with the Duchess de Vendôme, the sister to the king of Belgium who invited him to the Comédie-Française; his uncles, Jacques de

Fonscolombe and Maurice, Viscount de Lestrange; and especially, his cousin Yvonne de Lestrange, Duchess de Trévise, who often let him stay in her luxurious mansion on the Quai Malaquais, where a bedroom was available to him. It was two steps from the prestigious publishing house Éditions Gallimard, and Yvonne's living room was frequented by the likes of André Gide, Jean Prévost, Gaston Gallimard, and Ramon Fernandez, which would later play an important role in Antoine's literary career.

It was the fairly frivolous life of a young provincial aristocrat who was a little short on money but whose mother always responded generously to his incessant requests for more, making sacrifices in order to do so because Aunt Tricaud's inheritance provided her with only modest means. But Saint-Exupéry had to maintain his social status. He went to the theater and to the Opéra, took dance classes, frequented the brasseries of Saint-Germain-des-Prés, flirted with the sisters of his friends, spent nights playing poker or bridge, and became infatuated with some rather dimwitted young American girls. He continued to write poetry, hoping to seduce a young girl from a good family, with uneven success. He ended up being bored all the same. His best friends had passed their exams and had professional futures in front of them, while he was still searching for himself. He would have liked to have been independent, but he didn't have the means, so he depended on his family and, above all, his mother. His principal assets were his aristocratic name and the title of Count, which he had inherited after the death of both his father and grandfather.

Soon, he would need to visit another planet, which on the face of it wasn't all that exciting. But he went nonetheless to find his vocation, or at least one of his vocations—for he would lead two careers simultaneously in order to satisfy different facets of his complex personality.

In April of 1921, he was called up to military service, and perhaps because he retained the exhilarating memory of his air baptism, he chose to be enrolled into the Second Fighter Group, based in Strasbourg-Neuhof. As a private second class, he wasn't slated to become a pilot. After undergoing training, he would certainly have the opportunity to fly but only as a gunner; meanwhile he was a *rampant*—a "crawler," in other words, an insect incapable of flying—stuck on the ground and helping to maintain the aircraft and the runways. When he informed his superiors that he'd his passed his baccalauréat exam and had taken three years of courses in higher mathematics, they urged him to teach classes in aerodynamics. He requested and received money from his mother to rent a room in town, in one of Strasbourg's better neighborhoods, which allowed him to escape the strictness and the lack of privacy of the barracks whenever he had the time. He was often bored, complaining of having "nothing to do"; he felt like he was in a "big soccer camp," but the daily contact with airplanes and pilots rekindled his irrepressible desire to fly.

The passionate "crawler" would persuade indulgent pilots to take him up for acrobatic flights that would thrill him to no end. From that point on his ambition was to take command of a plane himself, but without having to prolong his army service, which he would need to do in order to take the courses required to obtain his military license. There was only one solution: obtain a civil pilot's license, which was feasible because, by a happy coincidence, the army shared the Neuhof field with the commercial firm Compagnie Transarienne de l'Est. Robert Aéby, the company's regular pilot, was available to give Saint-Exupéry lessons. Unfortunately, regulations forbade a serviceman to fly civil airplanes. Once again, Antoine was able to call on his family connections. By another stroke of luck, his superior, Captain de Billy, happened to know his family well and authorized Saint-Ex to train as a pilot on the condition that the training take place outside his service hours and that this breach of the rules be kept secret at all costs. So Saint-Ex took intensive courses—expensive ones, too, but Marie once again pulled out her wallet. Admittedly, with a young man's appealingly carefree spirit—and a touch of egotism—Antoine knew how to make himself both insistent and persuasive: "*Maman*, if you only knew how irresistible my desire to fly is—and it's becoming more and more so. If I'm not able to, I will be *very* unhappy. . . . You told me in your letter to make only a well-considered decision; I promise you that this one is. I don't have a minute to lose, hence my haste. I start on Wednesday no matter what, but I'd quite like to have the money on Tuesday."[8]

During his apprenticeship, he experienced his first aerial accident—from which he managed to extricate himself without too much damage—and obtained his civil pilot's license. So it was that in July of 1921 he disembarked in Morocco as an apprentice pilot in the 37th Aviation Regiment, based near Casablanca. There, he was soon bored. He hated the city and the countryside, and he had little in common with his fellow pilots. Fortunately, he flew often, and he met up with an old friend from the boarding school in Fribourg, Marc Sabran, an officer in the more picturesque and seductive city of Rabat. Sabran introduced him into musician and artist circles, where he was able to bide his time in a more familiar environment. In February 1922, he returned to France to study at the Avord base near Bourges in order to become a reserve officer, which he did only reluctantly, for he had no military ambitions. He had to take courses in meteorology and navigation, which bored him profoundly; military discipline was unbearable to him; he even found himself missing Morocco and architecture. He continued to write, poetry especially, and to draw, sketching caricatures of the characters he met as well as, already, many odd little fellows. He made a friend, Jean Escot, with whom he would stay in touch for years. He perfected his card tricks, played chess passionately, and tried, without great success, to learn hypnotism. When the officers-in-training were sent to Versailles for the end of the training, he and his friend Escot went to the nearby Villacoublay airfield every day, where they flew Caudron C59s—training biplanes—and, of course, he returned to Paris and his friends.

It was at this point that he would land on another planet—one that rather resembled Venus.

IN THE AUTUMN OF 1922, Saint-Ex fell in love with his first rose. She already prefigured the little prince's rose, not only because she belonged to a family that made their fortune in producing seeds—recall that the rose from the B-612 asteroid had arrived in the form of a seed—but also because she, too, was fragile (she suffered from hip pain, which confined her to bed the majority of the time), as well as capricious and ethereal. She would receive her friends while lying in her room on the top floor of her family's townhouse on Rue de la Chaise: a more touching and romantic setting would be hard to imagine. Her name was Louise de Vilmorin. Henry de Ségogne, who had likely introduced them, spoke of her in these terms: "She was poetry itself, poetry incarnate, charm incarnate, with the small face of a young girl. . . . She was like a daydream, like a wonderful vision, enhanced by an absolutely adorable chirping voice, very intelligent, very astute—she was absolutely stunning."[9] What's more, she was already writing poems and stories. How could he not be seduced by her? Besides, she would devote herself to the art of seduction her whole life, without ever hiding the fact. One of her quotes has remained famous: "I will love you always, tonight." She also said: "I have no faith in my fidelity."[10]

It wasn't surprising that Antoine succumbed, for in his unsettled life, he dreamed of finding a spouse. What was astonishing, on the other hand, was that she—a woman with so many suitors, adorned with all these qualities, a true catch—would have set her sights on this moneyless young man, a provincial aristocrat without particular ambition, who was rather shy and awkward, leading her brothers to cruelly bestow upon him the nickname "vague pachyderm." In the little world of Louise's friends, many were surprised. But he composed sonnets; he dedicated what seems to be an entire volume of poems (unfortunately, now missing) to this beautiful woman; he knew how to be funny and touching; he was a pilot; and he was a count.

In the beginning of 1923, the young Count de Saint-Exupéry and Louise de Vilmorin announced their engagement. Antoine, who was still a military pilot, continued to fly regularly at Le Bourget.* He had great fun taking friends up with him on flights that were more pleasant in prospect than in hindsight, for his passengers would find themselves back on terra firma shaken by the aerial acrobatic tricks that Saint-Ex

---

* Le Bourget, which today is in the department of Seine-Saint-Denis, was one of the first civil and military airfields in the Parisian region. It was on this field that Charles Lindbergh touched down on May 21, 1927, after his crossing of the Atlantic.

couldn't seem to give up. But on May 1, 1923, he took off in a plane that he wasn't authorized to fly, a Hanriot HD14. Due to his own error, the plane spun downward and crashed. The pilot and his passenger were badly injured. It was the first serious accident in a series that would continue for some time. Saint-Ex was punished—although with some indulgence, as the official report noted that he was "an excellent pilot, with passion"—and spent two weeks in the hospital. But the accident weakened somewhat his position with his fiancée's family. Louise's mother, who already wasn't particularly enamored with him—she wanted a more prestigious match for her daughter—was convinced that Louise was destined for early widowhood. Antoine was put on notice that he must give up flying. He promised to—he must truly have been in love!—and, that fall, he accepted the job his future in-laws found for him: he would be a "production supervisor" in the Tuileries Boiron on the Rue du Faubourg-Saint-Honoré, where he would be in charge of bookkeeping and filing. Obviously, it's very difficult to imagine him in such a position, and he thought so, too. In reality, he did very little, spending his days contemplating his watch and losing himself in daydreams.

Despite Antoine's willingness to make this sacrifice, the relationship between him and Louise, after countless adventures, began to deteriorate little by little. Louise would later speak of him with tenderness and emotion, calling him "the magician of our adolescence. A minstrel, a knight, a noble wizard, a mysterious child, moved to life by the whisper of grace."[11] But the time never came for them to marry—neither for her, as she realized she wasn't ready to lead a life deprived of the luxury she had always known, nor for him, as he was still searching for an ill-defined ideal and worried about Louise's frivolousness and inconstancy. Just as the little prince would later do, he chose not to do battle with the rose's whims. Their engagement was broken off in the beginning of 1924. The experience must have been painful for Saint-Ex, and he needed a lot of time to forget Louise, if he ever did manage to. The manuscript of *Southern Mail* was dedicated to her, although the dedication wasn't retained in the published version. This first novel, which juxtaposes two separate stories—one of hopeless love and the other about the opening of a new airline—strongly resembles an exorcism as well as an unsuccessful attempt to unite both the Saint-Exes: the one who loves the Earth and who would like to love a woman, and the other who dreams of taking off . . . a writer and an aviator.

Saint-Ex resumed his wandering. In the autumn, he quit his job at the Tuileries Boiron, which by his own account was about as right for him as "an evening gown," in order to transform himself into a salesman for a truck manufacturer. During the first three months, he had to master the basics of mechanics, learning to take apart and reassemble engines in his blue worker's overalls. This experience—being in close contact with mechanics, far from the Boulevard Saint-Germain and his sophisticated friends—enchanted him. Since childhood, he had always been passionate about mechanics: he loved the "realness" and the hands-on "doing" that didn't lie, was exactly as it appeared on the surface, and the simple frankness of his relationships with the other workers. Later on, he would happily find himself in a similar environment when he was hired at Latécoère.

But, after his training, things began to go downhill when he had to crisscross deep France—in Allier, Cher, and Creuse, three of the country's *départements*, or administrative divisions—to try to sell his company's vehicles. He may have been a fairly competent mechanic, but he was a very poor salesman. It appears that in one year he managed to sell only one vehicle (although even this hasn't been positively proven), while his colleagues would sell three or four each month. He went from hotel to hotel, from Bourges to Montluçon, passing by way of Vierzon, Guéret, and Argenton-sur-Creuse. He wrote often to his friends on the stationery of unlikely hotels, perfecting his gifts as a caricaturist by illustrating his letters with figures sketched from real life. But very quickly he became bored to death, writing, "Nothing happens in my life. I get up, I drive, I have lunch. I have dinner, I don't think about anything. It's sad."[12] In the autumn of 1925, after one year of melancholy immersion, he left Saurer and returned to Paris.

Once more, he found himself without any serious occupation. Thanks again to his connections, he did find his first job as a pilot, at the Compagnie Aérienne Française in Le Bourget, which specialized in tourist flights. Although this experience was useful for him in leading to his being recruited at Latécoère, the few aerial baptisms that he carried out from time to time were not nearly enough to support his way of life. Fortunately, his mother was still there—but he was beginning to realize that this financial dependence would need to stop one day. He drifted farther and farther away from superficial Parisian life, from the moneyed class of the *haute bourgeoisie* and its fake culture: its chatter, gossip, and pretensions had become unbearable to him. Time had passed, and he had gotten to know other planets—the army and its hierarchy, disappointment in love, accountants who resembled the businessmen and geographers the little prince would meet, the gloomy life of languid provincial cities, exchanges with simple men who made things with their hands. And grief, too: his favorite sister, Didi, had lost her child, and his eldest sister, Marie-Madeleine or "Biche," had died at the age of thirty. The world had changed, and he was sorry not to have really changed along with it. Despite the failure of his plans to marry Louise de Vilmorin—but had he been ready to take the plunge?—he continued to vaguely envision finding a wife, although these intentions remained ambivalent. He wanted a wife to keep him company and to assuage his anxiety, but he also was wary of "the mind-numbing comfort of marriage." He set the bar quite high, probably to be sure he would never succeed: as he confided to Didi, the lucky woman would need to be "beautiful, intelligent, charming, calm, soothing, and loyal." An ambitious challenge!

It was, however, during this period, when he seemed to have lost all grasp on his life, that his destiny—his double destiny— would come into play.

ALONG WITH THE POEMS and the sonnets whose purpose more than anything seemed to be to seduce young women, Saint-Ex tried his hand at writing a novel. He saw literature as a way to accede to his interior life, to discover himself and put confusion, superficiality, and easy, fleeting pleasures behind him. So he wrote, in snippets, laboriously, for he wanted to be honest with himself and not succumb to ready-made formulas or tricks. He first imagined the tragic adventures of a prostitute, Manon, who is searching for the One; but as expected, she fails pitifully in her quest. Good feelings rarely make for good literature, and this novel was no exception. But he had another idea, inspired by his experience as a pilot as well as his unhappy love for Louise. He imagined an aviator, Jacques Bernis, who constantly risks his life in the sky but also turns his gaze to Earth and its people. Jacques finds again a former love from his youth who is now married and a mother, and he hopes to tear her away from a sad, petit-bourgeois future. But destiny strikes and, after having lost her child, the woman herself dies. The pilot, logically, then crashes his plane. This would become *Southern Mail*, but it wasn't quite there yet.

Saint-Ex resumed his old habits in his cousin Yvonne de Lestrange's salon, which was frequented by many Gallimard authors. There he met Jean Prévost, an editor at the literary journal *Le Navire d'argent* (*The Silver Ship*). Prévost listened happily to Antoine's talk of his aeronautical adventures and, upon learning that he was trying to write, asked to read one of his works. Aviation was a little-known world at that time, surrounded by an aura of mystery; pilots were perceived as modern knights, and everyone celebrated the exploits of the "aces" of the Great War, like Georges Guynemer, Charles Nungesser, and René Fonck. Jean Prévost intuited that stories from the lives of these modern adventurers would appeal to lots of readers. At his request, Saint-Ex gave him a fragment, consisting of several pages from a novel he had been working on for months. Under the title "The Aviator," Jean Prévost published this short story in the April 1926 issue of *Le Navire d'argent*, alongside texts from the likes of Rainer Maria Rilke, Blaise Cendrars, and Marcelle Auclair. It was the first text published by Saint-Exupéry.

After two very depressing years, the stars aligned. Saint-Ex, who lived meagerly while he performed his aerial baptisms at Le Bourget airfield—helped by the money his mother would send to him—sought desperately to boost his income. It was suggested that he join the air force, but his two years of service had convinced him he wasn't cut out for the military, and he refused. He vaguely entertained the idea of becoming a journalist or going to China as a flight instructor and dreamed of winning the lottery, but none of this ever came to anything. He was feeling more and more isolated; his friends were embarking on professional careers after having brilliantly completed their graduate studies, and the Saint-Germain-des-Près set was becoming less and less bearable to him. And then a savior appeared, in the form of Abbé Sudour, one of his professors from the École Bossuet who had always encouraged his literary ambitions and with whom he had maintained a warm relationship. During the war, Abbé Sudour had become friends with an Italian count, Beppo de Massimi, a volunteer pilot who had become the general manager of Latécoère, one of the main aviation companies of the time and a pioneer of airmail. The kind abbey, knowing that Latécoère was seeking pilots to begin a regular line between Toulouse (the company's headquarters), Spain, Morocco, and Dakar, recommended Saint-Ex to Massimi. The two counts hit it off, and in October of 1926 Saint-Ex was invited to Toulouse, where he met Didier Daurat, the company's operations manager.

Daurat, a hero of Verdun and a squadron leader in 1917 known for his extreme rigor, intransigence, and apparent coldness, was entirely devoted to the accomplishment of a single mission: that the mail be delivered, no matter what it took. His ambition was to meet the challenge of distributing the mail every day, despite planes that were somewhat unreliable, atmospheric conditions that could prove extremely trying for pilots whose aircrafts often had only the most basic equipment, and sometimes the weaknesses of the men themselves. There was no indulgence in him: no place for amateurism or the picturesque, nor for romantic rapture. His pilots needed to exhibit professionalism, exactitude, and an ability to manage the demands of a job that was in the end ordinary: transporting the mail and sometimes passengers, and doing it on time, despite breakdowns and bad weather. Daurat often told the pilots, "Don't forget that fantasy and heroism have no place here. You are a worker."[13] If there was any grandeur in it, it was in the absolute priority given to a mission, even when the price to be paid was sometimes a man's life.

That the Count de Saint-Exupéry was recommended by Count de Massimi wasn't likely to impress Daurat. Nor was he impressed by the appearance of a worldly young aristocrat who, up to that point, didn't seem to have shone in anything, except in the salons of the Boulevard Saint-Germain. But aside from Saint-Ex's dreamy temperament, Daurat was seduced by his modesty, his desire to fly, his pilot's temperament, and his imagination. He hired Saint-Ex on a trial basis and, as was the norm, sent him to the workshops to be trained in taking apart and repairing engines. He was happily surprised by Saint-Ex's capacity to adapt to such manual labor, to make himself liked by his fellow pilots, and by his mechanical aptitude. In blue workman's overalls, Saint-Ex didn't hesitate to plunge his hands into oil and grease. Daurat wrote, "During the period where his hands, which such a short time ago had been so well cared for, were transformed, Saint-Exupéry discovered another side of life; a different man appeared."[14] In fact, Antoine was delighted by the whole experience. He rediscovered the atmosphere he had found when he was working on trucks for Saurer. He surely also rediscovered his childhood passion for engines, from when he had applied himself to building a flying bicycle—and too the appeal of, and his respect for, the fruits of men's labor—the exigency of real-life experience, engagement, and humble, everyday courage.

After several weeks, Saint-Ex was put to work testing the new Breguet 14 airplanes. Then he made several flights to Perpignan and flew as a passenger on the Toulouse-Barcelona-Alicante line piloted by Henri Guillaumet, who was considered to be the best of all their pilots. Guillaumet would become Saint-Ex's closest friend until his death in 1940. Finally, one day in the spring of 1927, Daurat summoned him and announced, "You'll leave tomorrow." Antoine was going to make his first mail flight. That evening, under a lamp in the dining room of the Grand Balcon (the hotel in Toulouse where the pilots stayed), Guillaumet indicated for Saint-Ex on a map of Spain—drawing in the mountains, valleys, rivers, and fields, complete with herds of sheep—that would allow him to orient himself or to touch down in case of engine failure. Their unshakable friendship was cemented over the course of that evening. Antoine, who as a child had very little interest in geography, wrote: "But what a strange geography lesson I received that night! Guillaumet wasn't teaching Spain to me; he made Spain into my friend. And little by little, the Spain on my map became, beneath the light of the lamp, a land of fairy tales. I marked with a cross the places of refuge and the traps. I made marks for this farm, these thirty sheep, this stream. I put the shepherdess, who had been neglected by geographers, in her exact place."[15]

In this way, the Saint-Exupéry we know (or think we know) was born in the spring of 1927, several weeks before celebrating his twenty-seventh birthday. He had discovered two planets for himself. There was literature: his short story "The Aviator," which had just been published, was the beginning of *Southern Mail*, which would appear in July of 1929. And there was aviation: he had officially become an Aéropostale pilot, and he would participate in the grand adventure of establishing airlines between France, Africa, and South America. He would never be fully invested in one or the other, because like everyone else, he wasn't gifted with the ability to be everything at once.[16] He would still experience many trials and tribulations—he would become a reporter, a lecturer, a "publicist" for the young company Air France—but until the end of his life, he would remain an aviator and a writer, or a writer-aviator. He would be *himself*, a person divided between the sky and the earth, between mechanics, including word-mechanics, and spirituality, the desire to unify his identity and to find a place, a source of light, within the mystery of Creation.

The teachings of *The Little Prince* illustrate this truth and this quest. He had approached an ending—he had sketched its contours—but the aviator, the author Saint-Exupéry himself, would shy away from its achievement. Perhaps its nearness was too much of a threat for him.

# 6

# THE VOICE CRYING IN THE
# WILDERNESS

SOME PRIESTS AND LEVITES from Jerusalem go to meet John, who
is preaching and baptizing in the wilderness of Judea. They ask
him who he is. After having denied being Elijah, John answers:
"I am the voice of one crying in the wilderness, 'Make straight
the way of the Lord,' as the prophet Isaiah said" (John 1:23). Setting aside any theological considerations and considering only
the symbolic dimensions of the two texts, we note that Elijah
is the prophet who will announce the coming of the *Mashiach*,
the "Messiah," at the end of time. In the Gospel, John "the Bap-
tist" witnesses the coming of Jesus, who is considered to be the
Messiah, hence the redemption of sins and entrance into a new
era: "Behold, the Lamb of God, who takes away the sin of the
world! This is he of whom I said, 'After me comes a man who
ranks before me, for he was before me'" (John 1:29–30). And
this occurs in the wilderness of the desert—the same desert
where Jesus, after having been baptized by John, spent forty days
before beginning to preach.

Saint-Exupéry himself became intimately familiar with the
desert in October of 1927, when Didier Daurat named him

chief of the airfield at Cape Juby on the northern coast of
Río de Oro. This was an obligatory stop for pilots flying the
route from Agadir, Morocco, to Saint-Louis, Senegal, both to
refuel and make repairs to their planes. It was in the middle
of nowhere, jammed between the ocean and the desert, a land
inhabited by dissident Moors who took stranded pilots hostage and sometimes killed them. Cape Juby was a Spanish fort
manned by about a hundred soldiers who were supposed to
keep the region safe, and by military prisoners who rarely risked
escape. Other than the fact that there was no place to escape
to other than infinite sand dunes, any attempt to pass beyond
the barbed wire surrounding their prisons led to almost certain
death, for the rebel Moors mercilessly slaughtered any foolhardy
"*roumis*" (Christian Europeans). Latécoère, the company that
would become Aéropostale, had constructed several hangars for
the airplanes around the walls of the fort, as well as a hut to
house the personnel. It was in this unlikely place that Saint-Ex
would spend more than a year, in charge not only of ensuring
the refueling and repair of airplanes and going out to help pilots
whose planes had broken down and were at risk of being taken
hostage, but also of a dual diplomatic mission. On one hand, he
was to improve the particularly tense relations with the Spanish, who were thinking of banning French planes from flying
over the Río de Oro; on the other hand, he was to build relations with the rebel natives so he could free the pilots who fell
into their hands and recover the precious mail. He would prove
effective in both of these capacities. He literally flew to the aid
of numerous pilots who had had accidents or whose planes had
broken down in hostile territory—this happened often—and
he negotiated skillfully in order to obtain the freedom of his
fellow pilots who had been captured by the rebels. He played

the game of seduction with the Moors, accepting their invitations for tea and inviting them in return, not hesitating to leave the protection of the fort in order to visit the chieftains in their tents, which until then no one had dared to do. He took classes in Arabic and interested himself in local customs, which surprised the local people but won their respect. Relationships with the Spanish improved notably as well. The commander of the fort, Colonel de la Peña, was flattered to have the Count de Saint-Exupéry to talk to, and Saint-Ex didn't hesitate to put his own life at risk by participating in the rescue of several Spanish pilots.

Despite these successes and the friendly relations that he formed with his companions and pilots passing through, including Guillaumet, Mermoz, and Marcel Reine, Saint-Ex suffered from his isolation. The material conditions of his life were extremely spartan: he slept on a thin straw mattress, his desk was nothing but a board stretched across two drums, and his furniture was limited to boxes of books, from the philosopher and journalist Alain to Victor Hugo and Friedrich Nietzsche. He wrote to his mother, "What a monk-like life I lead! In the most remote corner of all of Africa . . . It's total desolation."[1] Despite the peace he negotiated thanks to his diplomatic skills, he nursed no illusions about relations with the Moors: "They're thieves, liars, bandits, false and cruel. They'll kill a man like they would a chicken. . . . They'll tell you in all friendliness that if they meet you a kilometer from there, they'll cut you into little pieces."[2] He had plenty of time to perfect his card tricks, play chess with the Spanish, and write lots of letters to his family and friends, embellished with his usual little drawings. He tamed a chameleon, gazelles, and a desert sand fox: "I'm raising a 'fox—*renech,*' or a solitary fox. It's smaller than a cat and has immense ears. It's adorable. Unfortunately, it's like a wild beast, and it roars like a lion."[3] This story was accompanied by a drawing, in which it's easy to recognize the fox that will teach the little prince. He read a lot and wrote—painfully, he claimed, but when he left Cape Juby he took with him a 176-page manuscript: the text of *Southern Mail*.

Although he retained a bitter memory of those months of solitude and often of boredom—long hours spent in the barracks pressed between the sea and the sand dunes, threatened by the wind and by the Moors—he had confronted the essential realities of existence: the fragility and also the wonders of life, and the richness of the relations that human beings can weave among themselves. Didier Daurat would later write, "Saint-Exupéry grasped the meaning of the human mission, the potential miracle, which is to bring men together, to make them understand and love one another. . . . Saint-Exupéry's solitude in Cape Juby was both provisional and accepted. It was neither ennui nor despair; it allowed him to search for and to find himself. A new man was created in this isolation. From that came the detachment from all material possessions in this world, along with his unwavering devotion to seeking out the elevation of man."[4] Above all, he had encountered the desert— its magic, its mystery, and what it revealed to him about himself.

One day, it so happened that after a mechanical breakdown he was forced to land on an almost inaccessible plateau. Night had already fallen, so he knew there would be no help until the next day. It was then that he found on the smooth sand a black stone that could only have fallen from the sky: a meteorite. Much later, in *The Wisdom of the Sands*, he would depict God as a black stone. We'll return to this later. For now, here is what his fellow pilot, André Dubourdieu, recounted about the incident:

"Saint-Ex stretched out beneath the wings of the plane and fell asleep. Now, here is what he dreamed. . . . This stone reappeared, grew deformed, strange, not in its usual geological environment; it could only be some type of meteorite. In the dream, some eccentric people walked by, one of them more so than the others but very nice, who came over to place his pebble next to the sleeper and spoke kindly to him"[5] The desert, a sleeping aviator, a stone fallen from the sky, and a kindly little person addressing the sleeping pilot: this real-life episode from 1928, fourteen years before the exultant Saint-Ex would begin to draft his children's story in New York, is, with only slight differences, the beginning of *The Little Prince*.

But why was that memory so influential that it became the opening and the finale of his story? Why would he use precisely that memory to deliver his lessons to the world through the little prince?

When he left Cape Juby at the end of 1928 in order to take a course, at Daurat's request, in celestial navigation at the naval academy in Brest—the same school he had tried without success to attend in 1919—Saint-Exupéry already possessed all the elements from which he would forge the material of *The Little Prince*. First, of course, the essentials, as we've just seen: the desert and what fell from the stars that glittered so brightly above the immense desolation of the sand dunes. He also had the solitary fox with enormous ears, a sheep—there was no lack of them in the nomads' herds—elephants and snakes, baobab trees that had become emblematic of Senegal, and also a capricious rose that he had had to leave: Louise de Vilmorin. At the Boiron Tuileries and at Saurer, there was no lack of businessmen, nor of lamplighters assigned to repetitive tasks according to instructions whose meanings eluded them. In the salons and cafés of Saint-Germain-des-Prés, he met lots of conceited people, self-proclaimed kings, and drinkers. In the preparatory courses at the Lycée Saint-Louis, he was subjected to the teachings of geographers, or something similar—scholars who professed to know all without ever having been anywhere. He also encountered many hurried travelers who were "never content to be where they were," but who didn't know where they were running to, and vendors who sold "time-savers" that no one knew what to do with. As for the volcanoes, he would make their acquaintance a little later, when he flew over them several hundred times in Argentina.

At the end of September of 1929, Saint-Exupéry set off for South America, arriving in Buenos Aires on October 12. He was welcomed by Guillaumet, Mermoz, and Reine, the pilots he'd counted among his closest friends since he had become part of the "Company." Daurat had named him operations manager of Aeroposta Argentina. Saint-Ex opened routes in Patagonia and, up until 1931, confronted the raging Argentine skies, where extremely violent winds would make even "the stones fly." He flew tirelessly over the menacing peaks of the Andes and the infinite and desolate plains of Tierra del Fuego. He pursued the adventure he'd begun in Africa, complete with the dramas, anguish, and joys. He experienced what was probably one of the most powerful moments of his life in June of 1930, when he found Guillaumet alive and fell into his arms. His friend's plane had crashed in the Andes. After staying close to the plane for two days in the hopes of being spotted, Guillaumet had decided to leave and walked alone for five days and four nights without sleeping because he would have died of exposure, and without eating, other than some vegetation. Saint-Ex, after having

circled between Argentina and Chile—above the Andean volcanoes, in fog and in snowstorms, hoping to spot his fellow
pilot's aircraft but without success—had resigned himself to the
fact of his death. Who could imagine that a man alone could
reach the plains in the unrelenting cold, ice, snow, and wind?
The Chilean officers had advised him to give up his search, telling him, "It's winter. Even if your friend did survive the crash,
he didn't survive the night. Up there, when night falls on a man,
it changes him to ice."[6] Saint-Ex, in *Wind, Sand and Stars*, would
immortalize Guillaumet's superhuman courage as well as the
words that escaped his lips on rejoining his fellow pilots: "What
I went through, I swear, no animal would have done."[7]

*Night Flight* and *Wind, Sand and Stars* recount all of these
adventures, so there's no point in describing them in detail here.
Under other skies and in another role, Saint-Ex was continuing
to lead the life that had been his on the Toulouse-Dakar line
and at Cape Juby. He damaged several planes, as he was wont
to do, engaged in acrobatic hijinks, made surprising acquaintances, and was celebrated in the remote villages of Patagonia.
He frequented the fairgrounds, bars, and nightclubs of Buenos
Aires, where he appreciated the presence of easy, young, barely
dressed women, preferably blondes who spoke French. In short,
he was bored, and the trip that his friends Renée de Saussine
and Louise de Vilmorin took to Rio without giving him any
word that they were there—although they could easily gotten
together—didn't help his state of mind. He wrote to his mother,
"This is a really dismal country. . . . It is sometimes melancholy
to be always so far away,"[8] and to Rinette, "I so despise Argentina—where I live—and above all, Buenos Aires."[9] He was so
bored that he wrote, again to his mother, "Imagine, there is
no countryside in Argentina. None at all. You can never leave

the city. Outside, there's nothing but square fields, without any trees, with a shack and an iron watermill in the center. For hundreds of kilometers you see nothing but that from an airplane. Impossible to paint. Impossible to walk. I'd also like to get married."[10] This was an odd declaration of intent, bursting forth without any apparent link to what preceded it, and with no further details. This letter is dated November 20, 1929. Less than a year later at the end of August 1930, at a party organized by Benjamin Crémieux—the prestigious representative of the *Nouvelle Revue française* who had come to deliver lectures on French literature—Saint-Ex met Consuelo Suncin-Sandoval. She was a young woman of twenty-eight who had already been widowed twice—or, at least, so she claimed. He married her on April 12, 1931.

A NEW LIFE BEGAN for Saint-Exupéry.

He would leave Argentina, and he would experience many ups and downs during his career as a pilot, but finally he was married, to a wife he certainly could not have anticipated. He had just turned thirty, and he had been made a knight of the Legion of Honor for civil aviation. Éditions Gallimard, a prestigious French publishing house, had published *Courrier Sud* (*Southern Mail*), and in June 1931 they were planning to publish *Vol de nuit* (*Night Flight*), with a preface from André Gide, whom Saint-Ex had met in Yvonne de Lestrange's salon. The book would receive the Femina Prize. Tonio may have finally become an adult. From that point on, he was known as a writer and an aviator, and he was no longer obliged to beg for financial assistance from his mother, Marie. He wrote to her in 1930 after having just met Consuelo, "Bear in mind that of all affection, yours is the most precious, and that we come back to your arms in the weightiest moments. And that we need you often, like small children. And that you are a great peacekeeper, and that the sight of you is reassuring, as much as when you gave milk to your little children. . . . And it's a funny kind of exile, to be exiled from one's childhood."[11]

Clearly, Antoine was still waiting to meet the little prince who would reopen the doors to his childhood. Despite his travels, he hadn't left the wilderness. Despite the new landscapes, the new faces he would discover, the new experiences he would have, and even the war, he remained, perhaps without knowing it, an aviator asleep beneath the stars amid the desolate dunes, waiting for a child's voice, a prince's voice—that is to say, the voice of the son of a king—to call out in the desert and wake him up.

# 7

# ON EARTH AS IN HEAVEN

BETWEEN HIS DEPARTURE FROM Argentina and his mobilization on September 4, 1939, almost ten years passed that seemed to constitute a kind of erratic waiting period for Saint-Exupéry. In his professional and literary lives as well as in his personal life, he seemed to be trying his hand at a great number of things, starting out on paths but never pursuing them to their end, flitting between places and people. He continued his tour from asteroid to asteroid; the time had not yet come for him to return to Earth. It was a little bit like his own "Journey to the End of the Night." No doubt, his attraction for the sky, through his work as a pilot, was undiminished; but in part because of his own actions and in part because Aéropostale had undergone a court-ordered liquidation, he didn't really settle anywhere and passed from one line, one activity, and one employer to the next.

IN 1931, HE RETURNED to North Africa to fly mail on the Casablanca–Port-Étienne (Mauritania) line. (Port-Étienne is now known as Nouadhibou.) In 1932, he was a seaplane pilot on the Marseilles-Algiers line, which he considered to be like "a stroll over a lake." Air France, the company created in 1933, refused to hire him, so he became a test pilot for Latécoère—at that point only an airplane manufacturer—tasked with taking new airplanes for a trial run. There, he once again nearly lost his life. On December 21, 1933, he was testing a Laté 293 in the Saint-Raphaël bay. Having neglected to follow the precise instructions related to technical modifications in the plane's floats, he failed the sea landing. The plane flipped over and began to sink. Saint-Ex was stuck inside. He was saved by the engineer Vergès, who was assisted by several sailors in a rescue boat who dove in to save him. "After having helped him exit the plane, we also hauled him up onto the launch, half groggy and half drowned, for he had swallowed a lot of water," wrote Vergès.[1]

In 1934, Air France, showing its awareness of his fame, finally hired him for "propaganda" missions. In July, he undertook a mission to Vietnam that allowed him to see his sister Simone, who was living there; but when he tried to visit the site of Angkor Wat in Cambodia, the engine died, forcing him to make a crash landing on the Mekong River. Injured and running a fever, he had to be brought back to France. In 1935, having acquired (in rather mysterious conditions, given his deplorable financial circumstances) a Caudron Simoun, which represented the very best of aeronautical technology, he toured the Mediterranean to give lectures in Casablanca, Algiers, Tunis, Tripoli, Benghazi, Cairo, Alexandria, Damascus, Beirut, Istanbul, and Athens. In December, he attempted to set a record for the fastest long-distance flight, known as a *raid*, from Paris to Saigon, hoping to pocket the 150,000-franc prize. But he didn't take his preparations seriously and left on December 29 after having stayed up all night with Consuelo and some friends in Montmartre bistros and at the street fair on the Boulevard de Clichy. At 2:45 a.m. on the 30th, lost in the dark and searching desperately for the lights of Cairo (from which he was, in fact, quite far), he crashed his Simoun into a sand dune in the Libyan desert. Miraculously uninjured, he and his mechanic, André Prévot, wandered for four days in the desert and were saved in extremis, half-dead of thirst, by a caravan of Bedouins. In 1937, having acquired a new Simoun, he made several flights with the support of the Air Ministry, whose goal was to establish an air route between Casablanca and Timbuktu. He would remember fondly this mission, which allowed him once again to fly over the desert. In 1938 he attempted, again accompanied by the loyal André Prévot, a *raid* from New York to Tierra del Fuego, backed by Air France and the Air Ministry. On February 16, his Caudron Simoun crashed on the ground at the Guatemala City airfield, because he hadn't checked the fuel levels properly and had confused the Guatemalan gallon (4.5 liters) with the American gallon (3.8 liters). In his too-heavy plane, Saint-Ex was unable to achieve lift, and he crashed into a gravel pit. His new Simoun was in pieces, and he suffered a head injury, a fractured jaw and humerus, and various wounds. They even thought they might have to amputate his right arm. He remained in a sort of coma for five days, contracted infections, and stayed at the hospital for almost a month before returning to New York to convalesce.

That was the end of flying for him, at least until September 1939, when he would be called up to rejoin the Air Force in Toulouse. With respect to his writing, it seems that Saint-Exupéry didn't need to live like a real writer, meaning those who are generally in the habit of starting work on a new book as soon as they've finished the last one. Despite the success of *Southern Mail*, and especially of *Night Flight*, awarded the Femina Prize in France, he would wait until 1939—almost ten years later—to publish *Wind, Sand and Stars*. It should also be noted that this new book, which he struggled painfully to deliver under pressure from his American editors, was comprised mostly of a collection of old articles that had been somewhat reworked. But no matter: the book would receive the Grand Prize of L'Académie française and the National Book Award in the United States.

It was during this period that he began to devote himself to his "testament," the book he'd been talking about for a long time, saying, "I'm writing a poem,"[2] and that he wanted to have published posthumously: *Citadelle* (citadel) in the original French, or *The Wisdom of the Sands* in English. It was written quasi-Biblical style, evoking Nietzsche's *Thus Spoke Zarathustra*. Perhaps this hiatus from publication should also be seen as a consequence of the polemical response to *Night Flight*: many of his colleagues among pilots had reproached him for having used their adventures and the dangers they'd faced on every flight for his own glory as a writer—or perhaps they were simply jealous of his fame. Saint-Ex wrote to Guillaumet, "Because I've written this unfortunate book, I've been sentenced to misery and the enmity of my colleagues. Mermoz will tell you about the reputation I've acquired bit by bit, thanks to those who will no longer see me and whom I once liked so much. . . . So, life is now ruined, if my best friends have created this image of me and if it has become a matter of scandal that I'm still flying the lines after the crime I committed in writing *Night Flight*."[3] Certainly, not everyone had this reaction: notably, Guillaumet and Mermoz assured him of their support. But on the other hand, certain scribblers of the Saint-Germain-des-Prés milieu did find it scandalous that this book, written by a "sort of mechanic," was given a literary prize. "Just as the gentry of Saint-Germain-des-Prés considered grease unbecoming on a writer's fingers, the pilots of Aéropostale couldn't help but decide that a Femina prize winner must be pretentious."[4] Before *The Little Prince*, he would publish only two more books, which may be considered period pieces despite their literary quality: *Flight to Arras*, published by Reynal and Hitchcock in New York in February of 1942, and *Letter to a Hostage*, published by Brentano's, again in New York, in 1943.

Next, he tried his hand at journalism, the career he had imagined for himself when he didn't know what to do with his life.[5] In 1935, he went to Moscow for *Paris-Soir*, and his articles, which were lively and written in a distinctive voice, were a hit with Parisian readers. All the same, it has to be said that—in contrast to other writers who visited Soviet Russia at the same time, like André Gide or Louis-Ferdinand Céline—Saint-Ex appeared to be regrettably blind to the realities of the regime's criminal dictatorship. He wasn't shocked by the laws that forced citizens into assigned residences; he justified the existence of labor camps by the fight against delinquency; he didn't recognize the danger of a totalitarian regime that proclaimed itself in possession of the "objective" truth and brooked no challenge to that claim. In 1937, when he published several reports on the Spanish Civil War, again for *Paris-Soir*, he was no more perspicacious. This may have been because, as Virgil Tanase wrote, "For Saint-Exupéry, the grandeur of individual sacrifice was so glamorous that it canceled out the cause that justified it. From this perspective, to be on one side of the barricades or the other amounted to the same thing—which is noble, no doubt—but lent itself to confusion regarding the values one was defending."[6] This tendency to consider personal values and representations as metaphysical, in the literal sense of the word, while neglecting the realities on the ground, particularly the political ones, was surely at the root of his later controversial stance with respect to London and Vichy.

While we're on the subject of these journalism assign-
ments, let's note for the sake of anecdote that not only did
Saint-Ex meet a little sleeping prince on the train to Moscow
and ask a diplomat friend to draw him a sheep on a corner
of the table (a curious foreshadowing of the tale to come),[7]
he also barely escaped death—but for once, he wasn't at all at
fault. He was invited, alone and the first foreigner, to fly on the
Maxim Gorky, then the biggest plane in the world (forty tons
and eight engines, with a wingspan of two hundred and seven
feet), created by Andrei Tupolev. The day after this flight, the
plane crashed at Moscow's big main airfield, and its forty-three
passengers were killed. *Paris-Soir* had a scoop in the account by
Saint-Ex, recounting his impressions from his flight on board
this monster on the eve of the tragedy. In *L'Intransigeant*, he
published the story of his accident in Libya and his miraculous
rescue, when everyone thought he was lost forever. In *Marianne*
he published several articles about aviation; about his memories of Patagonia and Mauritania; about the end of "Émer-
aude," the Dewoitine D-332 that had crashed on a mountain
in Morvan; about Mermoz. When Mermoz disappeared in
the Atlantic on December 7, 1936, at the commands of the
*Croix-du-Sud* (Southern Cross), Saint-Ex paid homage to him
in these two newspapers. In 1928, in *Paris-Soir*, he published
three articles grouped together under the title "La paix ou la
guerre?" ("Peace or War?"), in which he exhibited a rather
angelic optimism, wishing that "giving meaning to men's lives"
would allow them to avoid a war that "would transform the
world into a cloud of ash."

He was also interested in the cinema. This is not at all surprising: at a very young age, he had been passionate about
photography, and his way of illustrating his letters with little

drawings representing the people being described reminds one of sketches on a storyboard. In 1933, *Night Flight* was adapted for the screen by Clarence Brown, Maurice Tourneur's former assistant, with John Barrymore and Clark Gable. The result wasn't greeted with much enthusiasm, and the *Vanity Fair* critic even deemed it to be "as terrible an exhibition of gaslight acting as I've ever seen in my life." Disappointed, Saint-Ex decided to involve himself more directly, so he wrote a screenplay, which he sold to the director Raymond Bernard. The film, titled *Anne-Marie*, came out in 1936 with Annabella, an actress who was a close friend of Saint-Ex's and would later marry Tyrone Power, in the lead role alongside Pierre Richard-Willm, who was an idol of female moviegoers at the time. Despite the boon of celebrity, the film would not become a classic. Graham Greene—and he wasn't the only one—found the subject "quite amazingly silly."[8] Saint-Ex would have more success with *Southern Mail*, for which he wrote the film treatment and the dialogue. He participated actively in its filming, which took place in Morocco. His assistant and script girl, a young girl of eighteen named Françoise Giroud, was destined for a brilliant career. He wrote two other screenplays, *Igor* and *Sonia*, both of which celebrated heroism, and there was talk in 1941 with Jean Renoir of adapting *Flight to Arras*, but these projects would never come to fruition.

In reality, it's unlikely that Saint-Ex was truly enamored of writing screenplays and making movies. He saw them mostly as a means of improving his finances, which were much in need of it. He wrote to Nelly de Vogüé in 1936, "Cinema and journalism are vampires that prevent me from writing what I really would like to. . . . If I throw myself enthusiastically into making these meaningless little movie trifles, I'll quickly acquire technical skill and will make a lot of money, but I take no pleasure in hoping for those successes. . . . I don't want to dilute my ardor. . . . Every screenplay, every article I write is one less opportunity to write a book."[9]

EVER SINCE HE HAD invented a flying bicycle in the park in Saint-Maurice-de-Rémens, or had taken courses in mathematics and physics at Saint-Louis, or had repaired the engines of Saurer trucks or Breguet and Latécoère planes, Saint-Ex had always been passionate about science, and even about pure mechanics—anything that combined ingenuity, human skill, and the laws that govern the universe. His sister Monot recounted, "His love for speculation would be developed in philosophy class. Did his love of mechanics precede it? Where did that first engine, which he would carry in a box like a jewel in its case, come from?"[10] It's hardly surprising that, when he imagined the meeting between the pilot and the little prince, it was a mechanical breakdown that initiated it; and the pilot finally succeeding in repairing the plane is what would bring it to a close.

Throughout the period of wandering, as he explored all the paths that seemed available to him, Saint-Ex gave free rein to his scientific creativity. He was interested in astronomy and in nuclear physics, but also, more prosaically, in the way planes functioned, and he set himself to tasks worthy of a true engineer. He registered no fewer than thirteen patents between 1934 and 1940, among them a new landing device for landing without visibility, a system to provide propulsion and lift, a new starter for the engine, and a new tracking method that used electromagnetic waves. During the war, he would surprise his colleagues by describing the possibilities for perfecting terrifying weapons using nuclear energy.

This restlessness, jumping from one activity to another, carried over into his personal life. It was as though Antoine at that time was similar to the gazelles that he caught and tried to tame in Cape Juby, which tirelessly and obstinately would bang their bodies against the fence, responding to a mysterious call from elsewhere. "They're captured young, but they survive, and they graze out of your hand. They'll allow themselves to be caressed, and they'll push their wet muzzles into your palm. So, you believe them to be tamed. You believe that you've protected them from the unknown sorrow that snuffs out gazelles without a sound, making them die the sweetest of deaths . . . but then comes the day when you find them pressing their little horns up against the enclosure, facing the desert. They're like the needle of a compass. They don't know that they're fleeing from you."[11] The desert, the "sweetest of deaths," and fleeing . . . this sounds reminiscent of something we know.

Nevertheless, throughout the muddle of those years, there remained for him one steadfast attachment: Marie, his mother, who was always present, loyal, indulgent, and generous. She had never let him down, and she would never let him down. Otherwise, the family circle had grown considerably smaller. After the death of his brother, the next victim was Marie-Madeleine, or "Biche," the eldest, who died of tuberculosis in June of 1927. The second, Simone, or "Monot," after having completed her studies brilliantly—in 1922, she was one of the first women to attend the École Nationale des Chartes—left to become an archivist in Saigon, despite Antoine's strenuous attempts to persuade her not to go, lamenting a separation that he was sure would be permanent. Perhaps because he himself felt a little guilty for living so far away—he was living in Buenos Aires at the time—he tried to convince his mother to dissuade her daughter from leaving. "And what a trap life is," he wrote to her. "Especially foreign lands, which will steal you away forever. You should know that all actions are definitive. . . . When a person leaves for Vietnam it's to stay there, even if she's dying of despair. And she can't make up for it by one day going on vacation to France."[12] As for his favorite sister, Didi, she had married and become a mother, and lived in the south of France in the Château d'Agay, which was owned by her husband's family. Saint-Ex went to visit her many times and would remain very close to her, his brother-in-law Pierre, and their children; but obviously, his closeness to Didi couldn't remain as it had been before her marriage. He maintained a close relationship with his cousin Yvonne de Lestrange, who had played an important role in the beginning of his literary career; later, when she was on vacation with André Gide near Agay, Antoine let them read the manuscript of *Night Flight*, which led to Gide's writing a preface for it. Up until the end, he would maintain a voluminous correspondence with her.

Saint-Exupéry's family constellation would soon once again be in mourning. In 1932, Marie was forced to sell the property in Saint-Maurice-de-Rémens—the château and the park that had been Antoine's refuge, which he would never stop referring to as a magical and benevolent place, where his roots and the poetry of his childhood were to be found, a sort of Eden. For him, it was a refuge that was inseparable from the image of his mother, who had given him life and protected him: "We felt safe in your house, we were safe in your house, we belonged only to you, and all was well."[13] While Antoine may have helped his mother move out, he never confided in anyone about how he had felt. He would make a pilgrimage there in 1938, but it was above all through *The Little Prince* that he rediscovered it, as we have already seen: "When I was a small boy, I lived in a very old house, and according to legend, a treasure was buried there. . . . My house was hiding a secret deep in its heart," says the aviator who has gone to look for water in the desert with the little prince, and so, "walking thus, I discovered the well at sunrise."[14]

PERIODS OF MOURNING, ESTRANGEMENTS, losses, friends who grow distant because they have their own lives to live—these things are part of everyone's experience. Children are born, people make other friends, those you believed lost return, new faces replace old faces, new lovers provide consolation for lost lovers. All the same, Saint-Ex had—finally—married! The union he had so long wished for had finally come to pass. "And so, I will be married, I'll have a little apartment, a cook, and a delightful wife," he wrote to his mother in 1922.[15] But despite his wishes, it was unlikely he'd fall into such a middle-class version of happiness with Consuelo Suncin-Sandoval.

Of Consuelo, who had already been widowed twice (or so she claimed)* when she met Saint-Ex in Argentina, every biographer paints a portrait that is more or less merciless, but apparently fairly faithful. "This happy widow, born among volcanoes and wizards, who exhibited her womanly successes as one displays the flags of vanquished regiments and who would tell at length over the course of an evening of the way in which she would make men drop like flies just by looking at them, had the soul of a courtesan."[16] And Saint-Ex dropped—knowingly,

---

* In reality, she had divorced her first husband, Ricardo Cardenas. But as one could not remarry within the church as a divorcée, she had claimed to be a widow in order to marry her second husband, Enrique Gomez Carillon.

it seems, although didn't he dream of taming creatures least likely to submit to being tamed? "One can be happy feeding a wild animal from one's hand, happy to give affection that is all the more noble because it's perfectly free, without any hope of recompense."[17] Consuelo was unpredictable, a mythomaniac, demanding, capricious, and jealous—even when she herself was surrounded by friends and lovers—and also an extremely extravagant spender. Saint-Ex exhausted himself trying to bend to her whims, and ruined himself trying to fulfill her desires— although admittedly he had never been particularly frugal himself. He spent entire nights waiting for her, searching for her in the nightclubs that she liked to frequent with her circle of admirers, for he was convinced that she was only a tiny being, fragile and lost, and that it was his duty to protect her. That isn't the image of her left by Saint-Ex's nephew, Frédéric d'Agay. "Aunt Consuelo de Saint-Exupéry, the widow of our uncle Antoine, didn't like children. I can't remember a single time she ever gave us a present. . ."[18]

It's not helpful for our purposes to linger on the chaotic— that's a euphemism—life of the couple, whose activities have already been much described and commented upon. Consuelo claimed she was the rose of *The Little Prince*, a claim that seems rather masochistic—frankly, that rose isn't very kind—but probably not consciously so. It suggests, too, a misinterpretation of the story. Consuelo, who couldn't see beyond her own egocentrism, believed that she was the rose because she saw the flower as the bearer of the essential meaning of this dreamlike story. *The Little Prince*, as she saw it, spoke about love, and of course, of the love she had inspired. Obviously, it does have to do with love in general, but about its deceptions and sufferings: it appears as a symptom of the narrator's relationship with himself and his own incomplete story, not as the heart of the message that Saint-Ex is sharing with us. If the rose does share traits with Consuelo—allowing us to understand why the little prince leaves her—it's also evocative of Louise de Vilmorin, the other woman Saint-Ex wanted to marry, and no doubt of other women he had loved, too. Perhaps it was even intended to evoke all women, as Saint-Ex saw them. . . . But is the rose really as important as all that?

In 1943 Saint-Ex, who wanted to rejoin his squadron in North Africa, met a young woman in the train between Oran and Algiers, a twenty-two-year-old nurse with whom it seems he fell immediately in love. This was not reciprocated, despite the letters he sent her—letters embellished with many drawings of the little prince, which spoke for Antoine via speech bubbles. Finally, Saint-Ex grew tired of her not answering his letters or his telephone calls, or showing up to dates he had suggested. He wrote to her, "But now I'm wounded by the rosebush while cutting a rose. The rosebush will say, Of what importance was I to you? I, sucking on my finger, which is bleeding just a little bit, say, No importance, rosebush, none. Nothing is important in life. (Not even life itself.) Goodbye, rosebush."[19]

In any case, although Saint-Ex was never able to let go of a strong sense of guilt from the feeling that he never did enough to protect "poor little Consuelo, so weak, so abandoned,"[20] the couple did in fact separate in 1936. Stacy de La Bruyère tells us that perhaps the pilot wouldn't have even undertaken the disastrous *raid* from New York to Tierra del Fuego if he weren't trying to flee his wife: "Madame de B. claimed once that Saint-Exupéry had undertaken this raid, which had no point and was in retrospect completely illogical, because his life with Consuelo had become unbearable."[21] It's not unlikely, but we must all the same be cautious when considering anything said by the woman called "Madame de B." This woman was, in reality, Nelly de Vogüé, longtime friend and lover of Antoine, who would remain loyal to him until the end. Over the course of years, practically until her death in 2003, she would conceal her identity with the aid of complicit biographers: Stacy de La Bruyère calls her "Madame de B," while Curtis Cate and Gallimard's edition of Saint-Exupéry's *Oeuvres complètes* call her Pierre Chevrier. This latter name is the same pseudonym under which de Vogüé herself wrote a biography of Saint-Exupéry (having known him very intimately), which was published by Gallimard in 1949. Virgil Tanase, in his biography *Saint-Exupéry*, which was published by Gallimard in 2013, uses her real name.

Antoine met Hélène (Nelly) de Vogüé in 1929 at the home of Louise de Vilmorin, who was a mutual friend. Hélène was the daughter of a wealthy manufacturer who owned important ceramic factories, which she took over upon his death. In 1927, she married Jean de Vogüé, with whom she had a son, Patrice, born in 1928, which justified her desire for discretion. Nelly offered Antoine a sense of stability that he wasn't able to find with Consuelo. She told Léon Werth's wife, Suzanne, that Saint-Ex may have behaved like a father with Consuelo, but with her he was like a child.[22] She mothered him and reassured him; she also used her connections in the worlds of media and politics to better promote his works. When necessary, she paid off his debts, and it has been said that she gave him his first Simoun. They took numerous trips together, notably to Germany and Morocco. She joined him in New York in 1938 after his accident in Guatemala. At the beginning of the war, she visited him several times in Orconte, France, where his aerial squadron II/33 was stationed, and then joined him in Algiers in 1943.

He wrote her one last letter on July 30, 1944, the night before his disappearance. In addition to the publication of a biography, Nelly de Vogüé would take charge of the posthumous publication of his manuscripts: *Citadelle* (*The Wisdom of the Sands*), *Écrits de guerre* (*Wartime Writings*), and *Carnets* (notebooks, not published in English). More than Consuelo, Rinette, Nada de Bragance, or Silvia Hamilton-Reinhardt, among others—even more than his cousin Yvonne de Lestrange—Nelly de Vogüé was the woman who, as much emotionally as physically, played the most important role in Saint-Exupéry's life for fifteen years. The exception, of course, is his mother, which perhaps goes without saying.

In fact, the relationship that Antoine maintained with Marie, his "petite maman," until the end, was extremely intimate: he bore an absolute love for her, and the feeling was reciprocated. It was as though—and he even confessed to this—he was still the little boy who dragged his little chair around in order to stay glued to his mother's petticoats. This is all the more surprising, troubling, or admirable—reader's choice—considering that they didn't spend very much time together during Saint-Ex's forty-four years on Earth. Marie did stay in Le Mans for some time when he was in school at Sainte-Croix, but when he was a boarder in Fribourg, Switzerland, their contact was intermittent, although he did pester his mother to visit his brother and him more often. Then it was boarding school in Paris, followed by military service in Strasbourg and Morocco. Beginning in 1923, he worked in Paris for the Boiron Tuileries before crisscrossing the French heartland for Saurer. Then there was Aéropostale, Dakar, Cape Juby, Argentina, Paris again, flying in Marseille again, Casablanca, etc.—and then the war, North Africa, America, and finally that last year in Algiers, Sardinia, and Corsica for the last takeoff. Before returning to America via Algeria and Portugal, Antoine paid a visit to his mother in October of 1940 in Cabris, not far from Agay in the Alpes-Maritimes, where she had settled in a little house after the sale of Saint-Maurice-de-Rémens. He gave her a radio set. They parted in tears. Perhaps they sensed that they were seeing each other for the last time.

Though they may not have seen each other very often, they wrote frequently, at least from the 1920s onward. In his first letters, Antoine began with "My dear maman," which was fairly neutral and standard. But sometimes he would use the formula "Maman whom I love," and at times, "Maman dearest," generally when his requests for money—which were constant—were particularly urgent, as in May of 1921 when he needed Marie to bankroll his flying lessons:"Maman dearest . . . Can you leave TOMORROW evening instead of Thursday to bring me the 1500 francs, of which you can deposit 1000 in the bank. . . . I beg you to send me a money order today, or to leave tomorrow evening instead of Friday. . . . This is all quite urgent, you know, and already I've lost so much time."[23] As was appropriate in high society at the time, he used the formal pronoun *vous* instead of the informal *tu* for his mother. With very few exceptions, he used the formula "Your respectful son" before his signature. Curiously, at the end of 1921, he abandoned "My dear maman" in favor of "My little maman" or "My little maman dearest," as though, now that they were physically farther apart, he needed to use a more familiar tone in order to feel close to her. This was the case up until the end—until those days in 1944 when he needed to use illegal and circuitous routes to try to get his letters sent. His last letter is dated from July 1944 (there is no exact date). "My little maman, I so want to reassure you about me and for you to receive my letter. I'm doing very well. Completely. But I am truly sad to not have seen you for so long. And I'm worried about you, my little old maman. How unhappy these times are. . . . When will it be possible to tell those we love that we love them? Maman, send me your love as I am sending you mine, from the bottom of my heart."[24] For unknown reasons, Marie de Saint-Exupéry didn't receive this letter until July of 1945, a year after her son disappeared.

In every letter, Antoine recounted his daily life, shared anecdotes with his mother, referred to his solitude, his desires, his pleasures—at least, those that could be spoken of—and his plans. He asked for money and often embellished his anecdotes with little drawings. Above all, these letters constituted long declarations of tenderness and love, the love of a son who saw himself always as a small child, trying desperately to regain the closeness, warmth, and security that only she, the tireless mother, could give him again and again, as she had in the past. We could quote them all, but we need only snippets to understand his emotion.

"MAMAN, I HAVE TO tell you how much I admire and love you, even if I don't express it very often or very well. It provides such a sense of security, love like yours, and I think it requires a long time to understand. . . ."

"But know, my little maman, that you have given sweetness to my life like no one else has been able to. And that you are the most "refreshing" of memories, the one that awakens the most in me. And the slightest thing of yours keeps my heart warm: your sweater, your gloves, it's my heart that they're protecting. . . ."

"You who are so weak, did you know yourself to be such a guardian angel, so strong and wise and so full of blessings, that we pray to you when we are alone at night? . . ."

"You can never really understand the immense gratitude I have for you, nor the house of memories you've built for me. . . ."

"My little maman, how can you wonder if your letters bore me! They're the only ones that make my heart truly beat. . . ."

"It seems to me that every day I learn to know you and to love you a little more. It's always true that 'mama' is the only true refuge for unhappy men. . . ."

"I cried reading your words, which were so full of meaning, because I called for you in the desert. I had been overcome with anger for the departure of all men, for the silence, and I called for my maman. . . . But it's you I needed: it was up to you to protect me and to shelter me, and I called for you, with all the egotism of a little goat. . . ."[25]

THROUGHOUT THIS WHOLE CORRESPONDENCE, written between 1920 and 1936, it is remarkable that the tone and what the words evoke remain the same: protection, refuge, safety, and intense emotion are mentioned, over and over. During all those years, Antoine lived through particularly intense experiences in the army, the desert, and the Andes; he met many people; he frequented places as different as the townhouses of aristocratic Parisians, the cafés of Saint-Germain, truck factories, and airplane runways in the middle of the Pampas; he had become a pilot and a writer; he had gotten married. It seems, however, that nothing changed in the relationship between him and his mother, as though it was impossible for him to distance himself, to consider the past as the past, and thus to turn what he had lived into memories. Antoine didn't leave his mother, nor his childhood home; he was inhabited by one and still inhabited the other. A part of him never grew up. And this eternal child, this little Sun King with his crown of blond curls, lived alongside the man who battled and grieved, who aged, who searched for his own truth and for the meaning of life.

Antoine didn't see his mother, Marie, as a woman, nor did he see her as simply an attentive mother. He saw her as the Mother, the one who raised the Son and who was "so full of blessings that we pray to you when we are alone at night." As for the Father, He was in Heaven, and His kingdom had not yet come.

# 8

# TRIBULATIONS

*"In this world you have tribulation; but be of good cheer,
I have overcome the world."*

—John 16:33

AUGUST 31, 1939: A false flag operation on the Gliwice radio tower near the Polish border, schemed up by the Reichsführer-SS Heinrich Himmler, was used by Germany as justification for opening hostilities against Poland. On September 1 at 4:45 a.m., German troops invaded Poland without a declaration of war. The same day, France and the United Kingdom ordered general mobilization. On September 3, the United Kingdom declared war against Germany at 11:00 a.m., followed by France at 5:00 p.m. The apocalypse had just begun.

On September 9, Captain de Saint-Exupéry was called up to report for duty in Toulouse, where he was appointed as a navigation instructor. Facing the imminence of war, he had returned to France on August 30 after cutting short his stay in the United States, which he had visited in July, and then again in August at the request of his American editors. Saint-Ex was convinced that war was inevitable. In August of 1937 he had made an incredible trip in Germany on his Simoun, in the company of

Nelly de Vogüé. Since he had completely disregarded the flight restrictions that were already in place over German skies, the French military attaché had to intervene as soon as he touched down in Berlin to spare him annoying sanctions. On his return trip, he did even better: having detected a suspicious odor in the cabin, he touched down, again without authorization, on an airfield in Wiesbaden. But as that runway was reserved for the future pilots of the German Air Force, the plane was immobilized, and Saint-Ex and Nelly were suspected of espionage. Luckily, Nelly spoke German well and had local connections. The ambassador of France himself even intervened, and at the end of the day, the "spies" were allowed to take off again. To impress the young German pilots who, out of a sense of solidarity with a fellow pilot, had supplied him with pints of beer the entire afternoon, Saint-Ex put the plane into a dive after taking off, skimming the rooftops of the barracks. The future pilots enthusiastically honored him with a Nazi salute. In March 1939, he returned to Germany, this time in a car, but again with Nelly. While in Berlin he met Otto Abetz, the German ambassador in Paris, who was trying to rally French intellectuals and writers around the Reich's cause. His arguments hadn't been convincing—except for the fact that the Nazis had put a totalitarian regime in place. In Nuremberg, he had seen members of the Hitler Youth parading past; in Pomerania, he had visited several *Führerschule*, schools of the National Socialist Party; he was awakened one night by a convoy of military vehicles crossing the town. Upon his return, he had no more illusions. He declared to the doctor Georges Pélissier, whom he had lent his apartment while he was away, "They're building so many planes that they don't have time to make hangars in which to store them. I walked along fields covered with aircrafts waiting in the open air. They wouldn't build so many planes and then leave them exposed to the elements if they weren't planning to use them right away. My friend, it's war!"[1]

Of course, as noted earlier, his position as a behind-the-scenes instructor didn't suit him at all. He wanted to fight, to put his life on the line. The military doctors declared him unfit to fly due to his age, the sequelae of his many accidents, and his frequent headaches—he didn't even tell them that he was often subject to inexplicable spikes of fever. He refused a post at the Center of National Research, which was offered to him in view of the numerous patents he had filed. He refused to work for the Ministry of Information, directed by Jean Giraudoux. He resisted the friendly pressure of Didier Daurat and Léon Werth, both of whom tried to persuade him that his role in the war would be more effective as a "moral reference" than as a pilot whose life would be seriously threatened, especially as he was too old to engage in aerial combat. But he saw himself as a shepherd responsible for protecting his herd: "When you're in danger, you feel that you're responsible for everyone,"[2] a principle that the little prince would share. He said that he was in despair at not being part of a combat unit, and he addressed poignant pleas to Nelly Vogüé that she pull strings for him: "If I'm not a part of the war, I feel morally ill. I have many things to say about what's happening. I can say them as a fighter, not as a tourist. . . . So, I'm suffocating, I'm unhappy, and all I can do is keep quiet. Save me. Help me become part of a fighter squadron. . . . 'Those who have value,' if they're the salt of the earth, should become part of the earth. . . . I want to join the war out of love and out of an inner religious sense. I cannot bear not to participate. Help me join a fighter squadron as fast as possible."[3]

Finally, his efforts paid off. Thanks to the intervention of the Minister of the Air, he was offered a position, not with a fighter squadron—he didn't really have the necessary profile—but with a large aerial reconnaissance squadron, the II/33 group that was based in Orconte, a town in northeastern France between Saint-Dizier and Vitry-le-François. He reported for duty there on December 3, 1939. His reputation preceded him, not only as a literary man, but also as a careless pilot, a reputation he quickly substantiated. He returned from his first high-altitude mission freezing, for he had forgotten to plug in his heated flight suit. If we add his age and his various disabilities to the picture, it's understandable that he was welcomed with a certain circumspection. Lieutenant René Gavoille, the instructor of the group (who would still be there in 1943), exclaimed on seeing him land in his faded uniform, "He certainly can't have come to fly!" But in several days their reservations dissolved, thanks to his modesty and charm. Lieutenant Jean Israël, who would become one of the heroes of *Flight to Arras*, would later say, "He tamed us," just as the little prince tames the fox in the story.

Saint-Ex had just entered the war. This engagement marked the beginning of a new life, with the long-awaited rediscovery of himself on the horizon. Once this had occurred, "it [would be] finished," (John 19:30), or as the little prince would say with his last words, "There. . . that's all," before taking off for the stars—the end of his voyage.

BUT BACK IN 1940, Saint-Ex was carrying out numerous high-altitude reconnaissance missions over Cologne, Düsseldorf, and Duisburg. They were not particularly pleasant. Many flight crews didn't return. He suffered greatly himself, thanks to his old wounds. At thirty-three thousand feet, the loss of atmospheric pressure would cause pain to return at the site of an old fracture; on top of that, he had bouts of fever, which he tried to conceal because "if someone in my group suspected me of having bouts of fever, I would have been sent back to my desk. . . . Since I couldn't complain without being forced out, I carried out missions at high altitude with a high fever."[4] On May 23, on board a Bloch 174, he carried out a mission to photograph the situation around Arras, which was threatened by the lightning offensive that the German troops had launched on May 10. His plane was escorted by five Dewoitine 520s to keep the German fighter planes at a distance. Two were shot down. Flying at low altitude to photograph the Panzer columns, his own plane was hit by an anti-aircraft battery, and one of his oil tanks was punctured. He managed, fairly miraculously, to land at Orly. It was the account of this flight that would inspire *Pilote de guerre*, published in February 1942 in New York under the title *Flight to Arras*. On June 2, 1940, Saint-Ex received a unit citation, the Croix de guerre.

By June 10, the front had been broken through, and the Germans were racing toward Paris. The roads were crowded with fleeing civilians who were being strafed by the Luftwaffe's Stuka dive-bombers. Saint-Exupéry's group retreated to Bordeaux, where the government had taken refuge. On June 17, Pétain requested an armistice. The II/33 squadron received the order to report to North Africa. The mess on the tarmac at the Bordeaux airport was indescribable, and Antoine, who was supposed to be conveying one of his squadron's Bloch 174s, set his sights instead on a Farman 220, a big transport plane he had never piloted but that would allow him to take along forty people, equipment, weapons, and . . . a dog. Among the passengers was a nurse named Suzanne Torrès, who was the future wife of General Massu and whom Saint-Ex tried, without success, to frighten during the flight by claiming that they were being chased by German fighter planes and that the plane was losing its rivets. After a stop in Perpignan, the Farman took off again for Oran, a flight that took five hours in the foggy, difficult conditions. "Saint-Exupéry piloted the Farman through a thick fog, out of which other planes emerged from all sides. It was as though the passengers were taking advantage of the migration of a flock of wild birds to cover their escape, just as one of Saint-Exupéry's heroes would later do."[5]

On June 22, the day when France surrendered in Rethondes by signing an armistice in the railway carriage used for the armistice of 1918, Saint-Ex landed in Algiers. The British attack on the French Navy at Mers-el-Kébir on July 3 slowed the breakup of the squadron. After one last reconnaissance mission on the same Bloch 174 that he had flown above Arras, Saint-Ex was demobilized on July 31. On August 5, he returned to Marseille, where he was welcomed by Nelly de Vogüé, who had rented a villa on the coast not far from Agay in order to be closer to him. It was there, in fact, that Saint-Ex spent the summer with his family, working on his masterpiece: his long desert poem, which he already predicted he would never finish.

What was there to do in a vanquished France, sliced in two by a line of demarcation that separated the occupied zone from the "nono" (non-occupied) zone? Many people, including Léon Werth and Nelly's brother, urged him to join de Gaulle in London. But the general irritated Saint-Ex, who didn't like the way he had condemned Pétain and Vichy. For his part, he was convinced that the armistice was inevitable because France, which had fallen prey to its materialistic demons, had contributed to its own downfall. Although individual sacrifice seemed to him to be necessary in certain circumstances in the name of honor, collective suicide would be pure folly. In his eyes, pursuing combat in 1940 on their own territory would have had no other result than the total destruction of all French forces. Despite the fact that many of his friends had endorsed Vichy, he didn't feel drawn to it, notably because the anti-Semitic measures put forth by Pétain revolted him. So, what to do? Continue to fight against Nazism—but with whom, and where?

Saint-Ex no longer had a "place." Saint-Maurice-de-Rémens, which had been so dear to his heart, had become a summer camp. Agay, where Didi lived with her husband and her sons, was a welcoming refuge but only a temporary one. In Paris, he had a studio on the Rue Michel-Ange, but Paris was occupied by the Germans. As for Consuelo, she had moved to Oppède, a little village in the department of Vaucluse, and lived in a sort of artists' community. Since he also was without funds in France, he decided to take a step back and go spend several weeks in New York, where his editors were asking for him and could be persuaded to give him advances. He consulted Léon Werth, who encouraged him, although he would have preferred that he go to London; but Saint-Ex definitely felt no sympathy for de Gaulle, whom he accused of wanting to divide the French. Werth gave him a manuscript in the hopes he could have it published in the United States and that he would write a preface for it. The text, entitled *Trente-trois jours* (*Thirty-Three Days*)[6] was misplaced by the American editors, but Saint-Ex's preface would become *Lettre à un otage* (*Letter to a Hostage*), published in 1943.

Saint-Ex needed a passport and a visa in order to enter the United States. He presented himself in Vichy to obtain them from the new administration, which had hastily been put into place; he would then need to go to Paris. Fortunately, Drieu La Rochelle, the new director of the *NRF* and a close friend of the German ambassador Otto Abetz, was also in Vichy, and he obtained a pass for Saint-Ex and drove him to Paris in his automobile, allowing Saint-Ex to avoid the crowded and unreliable trains. As they were passing over the line of demarcation, Saint-Ex, seeing the German sentinels snap to attention in front of Drieu's German-issue identity card, realized with whom he was traveling. For the future of his relations with the Gaullists, it would have been better if the pilot-writer had chosen another escort.

After a round of goodbyes, he left for Algiers on November 5, making a quick stop in Morocco before continuing on to Portugal, where he hoped to find a berth on a boat that would take him to America. It would have simpler to cross through Spain, but the articles he had published about the Spanish Civil War weren't appreciated by the Francoist regime, which refused him a transit visa. Saint-Ex would stay in Estoril, a seaside town near Lisbon, for a little more than a month. He didn't enjoy his stay in this unreal town where people organized parties, went out, and gambled at the casinos, while mingling with refugees waiting to leave, a town at once so distant from and so close to the war. He was still undecided and felt guilty for having abandoned his occupied country. He wrote to Nelly de Vogüé, "Tell me what to do. If I must return, I'll return."[7] It was also over the course of this stay that he learned of the death of Guillaumet, which shook him profoundly. Guillaumet was shot down while at the commands of an aircraft flying Jean Chiappe, the former police prefect who had been named the new French high commissioner, to Syria. Saint-Ex wrote, "Guillaumet is dead. . . . I don't pity him. I've never been able to pity the dead, but it will take me a long time to understand that he is truly gone—and I'm already so burdened by this horrible work. It will last months and months: I'll need him so often. . . . I don't have a single friend left in the world to whom I can say, 'Do you remember?' . . . There's a whole life to begin all over again."[8] Finally, on December 21, 1940, he embarked on the *Siboney* with Jean Renoir as his cabin-mate, and on December 31 he landed in New York. He would never set foot on French soil again.

# 9

# THE BEGINNING AND THE END

*"I am the Alpha and the Omega, the first and the last, the
beginning and the end."*
—Revelations 22:13

HIS AVOWED INTENTION WAS to convince the Americans to enter
the war. For this mission—which at the time he felt was the
only way he could fulfill his desire for combat—he was hoping
to make use of the popularity he enjoyed, especially since the
publication of *Wind, Sand and Stars*. But the stance he adopted,
which was for neither de Gaulle nor Vichy, wouldn't make life
easy for him, and what can only be called his ambiguities would
make it hard to get his message across, including to many of his
American friends.

The *Siboney* had barely docked when journalists began to fire
questions at him. He refused to say anything about Pétain, and
he expressed a critical view of democracy as it had functioned
under the Third Republic, maintaining that it had plunged the
country into paralysis and chaos,[1] a view that was very much in
vogue in Vichy. With his translator, Lewis Galantière, as inter-
mediary, he tried to "sell" American military authorities on
some of the aeronautical patents he'd filed as well as several

ideas, some of which were fairly outlandish, for invading North Africa. The OSS* didn't take this reserve officer seriously, especially as he obstinately refused to speak English.

More than these efforts, it was his writing, and in particular *Pilote de guerre*, which was published under the title *Flight to Arras* in February 1942, that would influence American opinion. The damning image of a France vanquished without a fight, which was the one largely propagated by the media in 1940, would fade in favor of the story of a man and his comrades in combat, a man prey to his doubts, emotions, and sometimes fear, but for whom the obligation to fight to defend his country and its values was nonnegotiable. It was a question of honor. Edward Weeks, a critic for *The Atlantic*, wrote about *Flight to Arras*, "The credo of a fighting man and the story of a great aviator in action, this narrative and Churchill's speeches stand as the best answer that the democracies have yet found to *Mein Kampf*."[2] The book was among the ten bestsellers of 1942. By this date, Saint-Ex no longer needed to plead France's cause to the American people and government: the Japanese had taken care of matters by attacking the American naval base at Pearl Harbor on December 7, 1941, precipitating the United States' entry into war.

After that, what purpose could Saint-Ex ascribe to his presence on American soil? He lived as though he had been exiled, separated from his family and from many of his friends. Nelly de Vogüé had recently joined him in New York in January 1941, but she had to return to France several weeks later. Consuelo disembarked in January 1942, which improved neither his morale nor his finances. He had affairs with several women, with

---

* Office of Strategic Services, the precursor to the CIA.

varying degrees of intimacy: Hedda Sterne, a young Romanian Jewish artist; Nada de Bragance, the descendant of dukes in Bavaria; Nathalie Paley, née Romanov, the granddaughter of Czar Alexander II; and Silvia Hamilton-Reinhardt, the young New York journalist at whose home he would write most of *The Little Prince* and to whom he entrusted the manuscript of the work when he rejoined the fight. He also evinced toward Anne Lindbergh, the wife of Charles and herself an aviator, a friendship that manifestly troubled her.

He had to defend himself against the attacks and sometimes the slander that he was subjected to thanks to his refusal to choose between the Vichyites and the Gaullists, who were tearing each other apart within New York's small French community. "Allied to nobody, Saint-Exupéry was attacked by everybody," wrote Stacy de La Bruyère. In 1941, de Gaulle tried to rally him to his cause, but Saint-Ex didn't respond to his solicitations, considering him a potential dictator and a divider of the French. He would never be forgiven.

IT'S WORTH EXAMINING THE fundamental reasons Saint-Ex gave for his rejection of de Gaulle. Certainly, he defended the armistice and thought Pétain was a sort of "necessary evil" to protect the population; certainly, he wanted the French to be united in service to their country, and he defended this rather idealistic desire, which stemmed from an admirable sentiment but ignored reality; and certainly, he couldn't stand the pseudo-Resistants of Fifth Avenue, who lived quite comfortably and were careful to insulate themselves from peril but who presumed to dictate what he should do. He wrote to André Breton, the French "pope of surrealism" who had taken refuge in New York and was quick to criticize any who weren't wed to the cause he defended: "You've been reduced to limiting your efforts to the strictly oratory. . . . I'm not 'condemning' André Breton. But the exercise of this very same freedom gives me the right to think that a 'right-wing' comrade who ought to have signed an anti-Nazism manifesto but instead asserted his right to die fighting Nazism—and who, moreover, is dead—is closer to me than any left-wing man who has carefully taken shelter. . . . You haven't known any Frenchmen who have accepted death. Now, I've known many Frenchmen who have insisted on risking death, and who have died. I believe in actions, not in grand words. My actions prove, quite simply, that my friends were worth more than yours."[3] But this anti-Gaullism was a knee-jerk reaction, too loaded with emotion—he would even become briefly angry with Nelly for defending the General's actions—to derive from anything but purely political or ethical considerations.

Among many other grievances, Saint-Ex criticized de Gaulle for speaking in the name of France when nothing authorized him to do so other than his own proclamation. Yet the pilot-writer truly worshipped his country, its people, the land—the ancient entity known as France that was for him the motherland. He established a true filial connection with it, a sacred connection like the one that bound him to his mother or to Saint-Maurice-de-Rémens. When it came to the fight to defend her, he would assume a mystical tone: "Our goals for the war! . . . Of course, the fields, the woods, and the evening gatherings in the villages, and the full barns, all that trusts in and counts on the future. . . . The stability of our heritage, this slow tradition we call religion, which little by little adds color to things. It's a slow color to build up, which means we have a magical world after several centuries of France, with our roots that extend so far back. We must have peace in order to create a soul, and the Sermon on the Mount seeps through the centuries."[4] Note in passing that, by evoking the Sermon on the Mount, Saint-Ex is making a reference to Christ that is fairly unexpected in this instance and that doesn't really fit with the rest of the text. But for now, let's return to de Gaulle, who provoked such resentment in our pilot.

Before June 1940, Saint-Ex, like nearly all French people, had most certainly never heard of this obscure colonel. At that time, he was just Pétain's ghostwriter and had published some interesting reflections on military strategy, notably regarding the use of tanks. However, these remained confidential and hadn't yet reached beyond the circle of the general staff and some political leaders. De Gaulle didn't make an appearance in the public sphere until June 6, 1940, when he was furtively named undersecretary of state for war in Paul Reynaud's government after having been promoted to the rank of acting brigadier general on May 25. But his famous "Appeal of June 18" made it clear that he would become part of history. Incidentally, it is very unlikely that Saint-Ex heard the speech: at the time, he had withdrawn to Bordeaux with his unit and was urgently engaged in finding a plane in order to reach Algeria. Thus, it would have been in Algiers and then Agay that he learned of the General and became convinced that he shouldn't join him, despite the encouragement of many of his friends, including Léon Werth and Jean de Vogüé, Nelly's brother-in-law. And we have already seen that this conviction would only grow stronger over time, especially in contact with New York's "resisters" and their schemes.

Be that as it may, it is somewhat difficult to understand the reasons for his immediate rejection of de Gaulle, since de Gaulle didn't stand for much of anything at this point and his plans for the future of the war—and, ipso facto, for the future of the country—hadn't yet been disclosed. The only thing that was absolutely clear and fundamental was that the General had rejected the armistice, which he considered dishonorable, besides the fact that a separate agreement with the enemy constituted a betrayal vis-à-vis the Allies, particularly England, which was continuing the fight. Logically, de Gaulle could do no more than accuse the French government of having betrayed its commitments and deny it any legitimacy. This decision was confirmed in October when Pétain, after shaking hands with Hitler in Montoire, called upon the French people to collaborate. Yet Saint-Ex was always very clear about his condemnation of Nazism; he was sickened by the measures enacted against Jews in July and early October 1940. He clearly did not envision the country remaining occupied by Nazi Germany, and he would do anything to be personally involved in the conflict. So, where did his instant rejection of de Gaulle come from?

At this point in his life, Saint-Exupéry seemed lost, prey to overwhelming contradictions. This is demonstrated in particular by the letter he sent to Nelly from Lisbon, in which he left it up to her to decide whether or not he should return to France.[5] What he emphasized in condemning the Gaullist strategy was that, on one hand, it divided the French; and on the other hand, and above all, that pursuing hostilities would have constituted a kind of collective suicide, since the population, no longer protected by the Vichy regime, would be exposed to merciless reprisals by the occupation troops. This was why he would never formally condemn the French state, going even so far as to tell his friends that "if Marshal Pétain didn't exist, it would be necessary to invent him."[6] He obstinately refused to take into consideration the "original sin" that made France the dispassionate accomplice to the criminal acts of the Germans, especially the deportation of the Jews, for which he attributed responsibility solely to Pierre Laval, the Vichy prime minister since April 1942.

This was the position that he attempted to justify in November 1942 with his "Open Letter to Frenchmen Everywhere" ("Lettre aux Français"), which was first broadcast on the radio and then published in the *New York Times Magazine*. This address, which began with a solemn "France First!" rejected any partisan or even political engagement and abstained from any judgment, even any ideological debate, in the sacred name of national unity; the only duty of the French was to fight. This text would earn him a rather biting response from Jacques Maritain, a philosopher and ethicist whom Saint-Ex admired and respected deeply. In Maritain's response, titled "Sometimes One Must Judge" ("Il faut parfois juger") and published in the weekly *Pour la victoire*, then under the direction of the journalist Geneviève Tabouis,[7] Maritain took the opportunity to question Saint-Ex's exaggerated indulgence toward Vichy, as well as the lack of realism of a position that, while advocating combat, refused to clearly take sides between those who collaborated and were willing to help Germany and those who embodied the nation's honor, however much they might deserve criticism, doubt, and even apprehension. In fact, "sometimes one must judge," and Saint-Ex would never reconcile himself to that. He stubbornly held on to a position that failed to recognize the strategic, political, and even ethical realities of the moment. The writer Françoise Gerbod noted about Saint-Ex and the controversy: "It seems that the fear of causing harm to French people still in France by a making a clear denunciation has paralyzed the expression of his thought. He is imprisoned in a position he has long advocated—that, if one hasn't shared or undergone a situation, one should say nothing—which must lead him to deny any value to the moral and political reflections of French people living abroad; he himself is living this in dramatic fashion, without any recourse other than to join the military again. . . . Inspired by his life as a pilot, and while moving as a document, Saint-Exupéry's 'Open Letter to Frenchmen Everywhere' is the expression of a tormented soul, whom no reasonable arguments can touch."[8]

Indeed, Saint Ex's position was not "reasonable": rather, it was affective, the instinctive expression of emotion. This shows clearly in his controversy with André Breton. He wrote to him, "Your point of view, which is as rigid as a policeman's, compels you to dishonor anyone in France who, in order to supply children with bread, must necessarily enter into a relationship with the Vichy government. You believe, with the severity of one whose stomach has been granted impunity, that such devotion to children would be a mark of disgrace. Let the children manage on their own and find edible roots."[9] Saint-Ex had already resorted to evoking children threatened by starvation during the lectures he gave in Canada during the month of April. He even went so far as to claim that two hundred and fifty thousand children had died of hunger, which was completely false. But did he deliberately lie in the name of his cause, or was he himself convinced, influenced by who-knows-what false story circulating in the exile community? Similarly, it isn't possible to believe that he could have reasonably imagined it would be acceptable to let the Americans and English determine France's political organization after liberation, as he seems to suggest in his "Open Letter to Frenchmen Everywhere." Can we credit that he was convinced all political and moral reflections would have to be eliminated as a source of disunity and that instead the French should simply take up arms?

It was as though, over the course of his two years in America, Saint-Ex had descended into his own personal apocalypse. In this existential torment, how surprising is it that the most primitive emotions and affects ended up taking control, compelling him to hate a man who tried to reconcile with him, to defend unrealistic positions against even his close friends, and finally to choose the extreme solution: returning to combat even though he was hardly in a shape to fight, with his own end as the highly probable outcome?

And so he found himself nowhere. The United States didn't appeal to him; he felt uprooted (and we know how often he used the image of a tree as a metaphor for life), for he no longer had a home, either real (he moved constantly) or symbolic (he no longer really lived with Consuelo nor with his mistresses). His France-motherland was enslaved, but she had her herald, whom he would call the "Great Mogul" ("grand Mogol")—de Gaulle, who had "married" her, or worse, who claimed to embody her. He was no longer writing, or at least he was no longer publishing, other than the occasional piece about the circumstances of the war; even *Wind, Sand and Stars (Terre des hommes)*, as we saw, is essentially a repurposing of older texts. No doubt, he was still working on his posthumous masterpiece, but what meaning could he give writing that he knew would never be published during his lifetime? He was no longer flying, and not only were the majority of his friends gone to him—they were prisoners in occupied territories or dead—but he was under constant attack, the object of slander by those whose cause he hadn't rallied to. Most notably, the rumor was spread that he had been named to the National Council set up by the Vichy government, and he had to call a press conference and threaten legal action to end the rumor—which didn't prevent it from popping up again later on, in 1944, when he left for Algiers.

In sum, his life seemed like a nightmare to him. "My life is in chaos, and there's hardly anything I can do about it. . . . A telephone call, a forgotten appointment, a check I must cash if I want any money, and all my plans change. . . . I am in such despair over missed trains, missed appointments, lost addresses, bills, forgotten phone calls, reproaches, difficult reconciliations, wounded friends, headaches when I have to speak, a blank mind when I have to write, three dinner invitations accepted for the same evening. . . . I've been living in two rooms along with the movers, my wife, and her friends, my secretary typing away in a corner, a cook who has gone mad and makes scenes, telephones and visitors interrupted by events outside. I receive [visitors] as though in the lobby of a train station."[10]

He thought he'd hit bottom in April 1942 when, having gone to Montreal for two days to give a lecture, he found himself stuck in Canada because his exit visa from the United States hadn't been validated. He was told it might take six months for the problem to be resolved. He called on all his connections to try to extricate himself from the situation, inundating them with letters and telephone calls, either desperate or angry: he was convinced he was the victim of a Gaullist plot. He managed to exhaust the patience of Elizabeth Reynal, the wife of his editor, by begging her nonstop to intervene with the State Department. He stayed in his hotel room, brooding over his bad luck and cursing the Gaullists and the American government. He somatized his unhappiness: he was unable to sleep and spent two weeks lying on his bed with a bag of ice on his stomach to numb pain that was probably due to an inflamed gallbladder. During this time, Consuelo, who had refused to go to Montreal with him, hired a private detective, convinced he was with another woman. She finally joined him, but that didn't exactly improve the situation. In the end, the two days turned into five weeks, and he lived this misadventure as though it were torture, which only worsened his paranoia that he was abandoned, alone, and surrounded by plotters conspiring against him.

He felt old and actually was in poor condition, thanks in part to his old wounds but also to a lifestyle his doctors wouldn't have recommended. He spent his nights writing and waking up his entourage to read them what he had written; he drank a lot, smoked endlessly, got no physical exercise, and took no care in what or when he ate. "I'm forty-two years old. I've been in a bunch of accidents. I can't even jump with a parachute. Two days out of three, my liver gives me trouble. . . . Ever since a fracture in Guatemala, my ear rings night and day. . . . I feel so, so weary! In the state that I'm in, I can't even carry a two-kilogram box, get out of bed, or pick a tissue up from the ground without suffering physically."[11] It was only in the company of other pilots passing through New York that he seemed able to recover a true *joie de vivre*. His translator, Lewis Galantière, wrote, "I've only seen him deeply happy, relaxed, without a shadow of reticence, on one occasion. It was the day he went to lunch with a group of friends comprised of only pilots, military and civil, who by chance had met up in New York. . . . His eyes shone, he was radiating happiness. He was like a child who was grateful to his elders for letting him play with them. He had rediscovered his childhood and joy."[12]

He wanted to fight, but no one wanted him to reenlist. His circumstances and the way he responded to them seemed to have closed him in a trap, in which he turned around and around like a lion in a cage. But this trap wasn't only the result of war and exile; it was also inside him. And it was because the outside world prevented him from "taking action" that he realized perhaps that the oneness of humanity, which he stubbornly extolled as the essential condition of freedom—because it freed up internal conflicts that had no solution—was also his own oneness, which he needed to find. "If it weren't for that difficult voyage, I would not be able to distinguish in myself, for better or for worse, the person I'm fighting from the man I'm trying to become."[13]

And so it was also a beginning.

# IO

## *ET VERBUM CARO FACTUM EST**

*For my life is spent in sorrow,*
*and my years with sighing;*
*my strength fails because of my misery,*
*and my bones waste away.*

*I am the scorn of all my adversaries,*
*a horror to my neighbors,*
*an object of dread to my acquaintances;*
*those who see me in the street flee from me.*
*I have passed out of mind like one who is dead;*
*I have become like a broken vessel.*
*Yea, I hear the whispering of many—*
*terror on every side!*

—Psalm 31:10-13

SAINT-EXUPÉRY NEVER REVEALED HIMSELF to be particularly religious. After he left his very Catholic family circle, we don't know whether he frequented churches or other places of

---

\* "And the word became flesh" (John 1:14).

worship. But if by chance he happened to hear or read Psalm 31, it's a safe bet he would have identified with it. There was his "sorrow" and his bones that had "waste[d] away" due to fracture; there was the way people tried to "pass [him] out of mind" by hindering his efforts to join the fight; and there was the "scorn" and "whispering" that surrounded him. How could he extricate himself from this dejection he felt in exile, so painful it was almost unbearable? He was like the gazelles in Cape Juby who were magnetically attracted to the desert—but how could he himself leave the enclosure?

AS IS THE CASE for everyone, when our relationship to the other—meaning all that is exterior to ourselves, the outside world—becomes deadly, we really have only two options: to change the other by leaving, altering our world and our way of life; or else to change ourselves, so that this other becomes bearable. This was the dilemma that Saint-Ex found himself facing in 1942. He had already written to Nelly de Vogüé, "I'm up to my neck in contradictions. Either I will die, or I will see clearly inside myself."[1] In one of the famous notebooks that he always carried with him, and in which he would jot down a wide range of reflections, he wrote, "A man wants to express what he experiences. If he doesn't express it, he comes up with a plan of action."[2]

This was, indeed, exactly what he tried to do. His plan of action was to attempt to leave and fight; as for self-expression, he continued to work on what he considered to be his philosophical testament, which at the time he had titled *The Tribal Chief* (*Le Caïd*) and which would become *The Wisdom of the Sands* (*Citadelle*). Saint-Exupéry thought of this work as a Bible—whose style he had borrowed, in fact—a last message addressed to all men, expressing a complete truth, his own truth, finally discovered and formulated: Saint-Exupéry himself, finally. His preoccupation with passing on an entire philosophy, evoking an element of scholasticism, was not new; aside from his occasional writings, it had even become the only work that mattered to him. In 1940, explaining why he had refused to respond to requests that he speak over the airwaves, he wrote to Nelly de Vogüé, "I don't want to speak on the radio; it's indecent if one does not have a Bible to offer people."[3]

Several times, he also compared his writing to a tree. "I feel threatened, vulnerable, pressed for time, I want to finish my tree. Guillaumet is dead, I want to finish my tree quickly,"[4] he wrote, again to Nelly. This tree symbolized the essential Being: a perfect unity with roots, a trunk, and branches. Thus, in his elegy to Mermoz, he wrote, "You were a tree with deep roots. Your anger reached far into the tuff. You let yourself be swayed by the wind."[5] In order for this tree to finally be finished, everything had be in place, sketched out down to the roots. And this tree—this definitive book—was nothing other than a projection of himself, as he revealed in another letter to Nelly: "I would like to be eaten by a tree. Then one would be able to feel all the birds that one protects."[6] And Saint-Ex knew that he hadn't yet brought together everything he needed to complete his tree. "There is a verity higher than the utterances of our intelligence. Something passes through us and governs us, which I experience without yet understanding it. A tree has no language. We are part of a tree," he wrote in *Flight to Arras.*[7] Because it is a perfect representation of Being, a tree bears a meaning well beyond intelligence, beyond what is reasonable or merely visible—and this is not far from a more poetic declaration: "One can only see well with the heart." He said this explicitly in a letter to

Nelly at the beginning of the war, when he wanted to return to the front and was still waiting to move past his basic need to understand: "Among the airline pilots, I'm a little bit like the earth that nourishes the tree. I no longer need to understand. The meaning of the earth, then, is the tree."[8]

This magnum opus would turn a little seed—"that came from who knows where"[9]—into a big tree that would be nothing less than "the meaning of the earth." Saint-Exupéry saw it as a cathedral, another metaphor he used often like the tree. And yet, there are no cathedrals that weren't built as prayers to God. The unbeliever would nourish his tree in this way: with a "spiritual," or, in truth, frankly religious and, more precisely if perhaps unwittingly, a Christian earth. His tree grew in consecrated ground.

One has only to read *The Wisdom of the Sands* to become convinced of this, for its tone and imagery are biblical, as Saint-Exupéry was well aware. "The only vocabulary I have to express myself is religious. I've come to understand this on rereading my *Caïd*; its meaning is impossible to formulate, but that's no coincidence," he wrote to Nelly de Vogüé.[10] No coincidence, indeed; and both nature and manmade structures are part of a transcendental principle: "The particles that make up the earth do not come together by chance and rise up into a tree. To create the tree, you had to first cast the seed in which it slept. It came from above and not from below. Your pyramid has no meaning unless it ends in God. For He will spread upon men once He has transfigured them."[11] These evocations—it's tempting to call them invocations, given the Biblical aroma—can be found in practically all his writing but nowhere more densely than in *The Wisdom of the Sands*. There are abundant examples, and it would be tedious to list them all, so a few quotations will suffice. For example, this is the last sentence of *Flight to Arras*—a single sentence that comes without apparent link to what precedes it, which is separated from the rest of the text by an asterisk, and is clearly inspired by Scripture: "Only the Spirit, if it breathes on the clay, can create Man."[12]

SAINT-EX WAS PROBABLY CONSCIOUS of the omnipresent religious landscape that imposed itself on him without him laying claim to it. He was surprised not to believe, when he wrote about a visit to a church chanced upon while he was out for a walk in Fourvière, a district of Lyon. "It's quite strange that I don't have faith. One loves God without hope: that would suit me quite well. Solesmes and Gregorian chants. Plainchant, the open sea . . . The church was empty except for the choir. And I found myself absolutely in a ship. The choir was the ship's crew, and I the passenger. Oh, a very secret passenger. And I had the impression of having slipped in there, a complete stowaway. And I was—this was it—dazzled. Dazzled by the obviousness, which I will never again be able to capture."[13]

One cannot consider Saint-Exupéry to be a believer, much less a Catholic. However, in his first book, *Southern Mail*, the hero—whom no one doubts is Saint-Ex himself—undergoes an experience that could have led him to conversion, just like Paul Claudel who was suddenly "seized" by the Catholic faith at the Cathedral of Notre-Dame on Christmas Day in 1886. The account that Claudel wrote of it in 1913 is famous. "I myself was standing in the crowd, near the second pillar by the entrance to the choir, to the right on the side of the sacristy. And that was where the event occurred that would dominate the rest of my life. In an instant, my heart was touched, and I believed."[14] Saint-Ex may have been inspired by that experience when he recounted Bernis's. "As he was passing by Notre-Dame, he entered. He was surprised by the density of the crowd and took refuge against a pillar." But the passage that follows, which is not without some ambiguity, is different. "He also felt the need to truly see himself, and he offered himself up to faith as he might to any other discipline of thought. He said to himself: 'If I discover words that explain me, that resemble me, then they will be true for me.' Then he added wearily: 'And yet, I won't believe them.'"[15] It was as though Saint-Ex, searching for himself, for a sense of oneness and his truth, wanting to express and to unify himself, had turned toward a transcendence—toward this Spirit beyond intelligence—but decided beforehand to elude it: "And yet, I won't believe them." In this way, beginning with his first novel, he expressed what would become his life's quest: "to reach the inaccessible star," just as Jacques Brel would later sing in his famous song "The Quest" ("La quête"): "Aimer jusqu'à la déchirure, aimer, même trop, même mal, tenter, sans force et sans armure, d'atteindre l'inaccessible étoile" ("Love until destruction, love, even too much, even badly, try, without force and without armor, to reach the inaccessible star"). At the end of Saint-Ex's life, this quest was still present, always the same. "There is but one problem, and one only, in the whole world," he wrote in his "Letter to General X." "To give humankind a spiritual significance. Spiritual concerns. To rain on them something that resembles a Gregorian chant. . . . One can no longer live without poetry, color, or love. . . . There is but one problem, and one only: to rediscover that there is a life of the spirit, higher still than a life of intelligence. The only one able to satisfy man."[16]

For all of his days, Saint-Exupéry seemed to stand at the entrance to the Temple. He knew—or at least he sensed—that it was there he would find the Spirit, a light that would restore him; but he didn't dare or didn't know how to knock on the door. This Spirit would remain undefinable, unrepresentable for him, and he mocked the pious images that claimed to represent it: "It is not in keeping with Thy dignity, nor Thy solicitude, to visit me on my level, nor do I expect anything of the puppet show of apparitions of archangels."[17] When he imagined a meeting with "He who is"[18]—taking here the definition that the God of the Bible gives to himself, "I am who I am" (Exodus 3.14)—he is confronted by inert black granite and nothing more: "Obstinately, I climbed towards God to ask him the wherefore of things. . . . But on the summit of the mountain, I discovered only a heavy block of black granite—which was God."[19] This passage in *The Wisdom of the Sands* is clearly inspired by the episode of the burning bush; yet, although on the summit of "Horeb, the mountain of God," Moses saw in the bush that "was not consumed" (Exodus 2.2) the light of an eternal fire, Saint-Exupéry saw only a black and heavy stone. The image is terrifying. One cannot help but think of the words of Frances Tustin, an English psychoanalyst who, during a conference on autism, recounted the words of a child who had suffered from this pathology, explaining the way he lived in the world when he was sick: "It was a black hole with a nasty needle in the middle." What, then, was this cold, inert, heavy black granite? Why did Saint-Ex—who was able to perceive warmth, lightness, and all of life's colors, who glorified (sometimes very explicitly, often in an allusive fashion) this Spirit who unified and provided the "meaning of the earth"—seem to be its prisoner? What does this rock—which, like Sisyphus, he seemed condemned to push without respite up to the top of the mountain, only to have it roll back down again—represent?

Saint-Exupéry knew he needed to give a certain face to this transcendence in order to access this Spirit that would liberate him, marking his success and the end of his wanderings—his own and those of all men, who were "eternal nomads, marching toward God," as he wrote in *The Wisdom of the Sands*. And he returned once again to a familiar metaphor: "God is as real as a tree, although more difficult to read."[20] As we have seen, he made the tree a representation of the finished subject, of his finished self; and it is therefore by God, or by a perceptible evocation of God, that he must pass, *volens nolens*. "If you had found God, you would have become a part of Him, and you would be fulfilled."[21]

It so happens that Christianity, a tradition in which he had been raised but from which he had obviously strayed, offered a way to access this divinity—a divinity that remains invisible and unrepresentable in Judaism, and whose name cannot be spoken. The Christian "revolution" is fundamentally based on incarnation, for the Word became flesh through the body of Jesus of Nazareth, the son of God who assumed a face and lived among men. And Saint-Ex sensed that there was this path through the incarnated Word; he brushed against it when, for example, he spoke of this "march toward God, who alone can satisfy you, for by following from sign to sign you will reach Him, He who is the meaning of the book whose words I have spoken."[22] The words—those he spoke—must themselves become flesh, or must at least become accessible images. Is this not what Saint-Ex had always done? He who challenged the importance of disembodied words, who saw value only in physical engagement—in risking one's body, one's blood, one's life? In fact, he explicitly drew a link to incarnation in the Christian sense of the term, as the only possible expression of the speech, of the

Word: "Nobody has the right to write a word today who does not participate to the fullest in the agony of his fellow human beings. If I did not resist with my life, I would be unable to write. And what holds true for this war must hold true for everything. The Christian idea of the Word made Flesh has served. One must write but with one's body."[23] When he pronounced these words in June 1940, Saint-Ex had just resisted with his own life, and he was therefore authorized to write about combat; this would become *Flight to Arras*. Nothing new in that progression: everything he had written up to that point was a literary translation of what he had lived. Nonetheless, all of this still did not signify a liberating outcome, or the end of wandering by way of an accession to the Spirit.

Although he never specifically wrote about it, he would retain and often evoke this feeling of exile: exile in the world, exile in "his" world. He eluded any categorization, and thus any sense of integration. He was an aristocrat and a blue-collar worker, a pilot and a writer, a man of action and a philosopher, worldly and anchorite, mystic and a sensualist. . . . But he was also in exile from himself, for a part of him remained separated, lost, as though he was lacking an earthly Eden in which he could put himself together again. In 1930, in a letter to his mother, he wrote, "And it's a funny kind of exile, to be exiled from your childhood."[24] This childhood, to which he no longer had access, was his native land. It was the formative place that he needed to take ownership of again, the place he had for so long been trying to revisit by drawing a funny little man over and over again, who floated here and there among his letters, his notes, and his restaurant bills—this child who resembled an angel, flying from place to place and from moment to moment, who accompanied him, faithfully and enigmatically, all throughout his life. And this child vaguely brought him closer to another child, who has been rendered immortal through his memory: "The world's recognition of a small child's birthday is a completely remarkable thing. Two thousand years later! The human species knows that it must make its miracle, as the tree makes its fruit. . . ."[25]

IT WAS AT THE end of his life, in the summer of 1942, at the point when he could have adopted for himself the words from Psalm 31 mentioned above, that the path leading him back to his childhood appeared. Through his drawings, it became possible to incarnate the Word that had so haunted him, and that he had tried for so long to bring forth in his magnum opus, while despairing of ever being able to manage it. Let's recall what he had written several months earlier, in *Flight to Arras*: "If it weren't for that difficult voyage, I would not be able to distinguish in myself, for better or for worse, the person I'm fighting from the man I'm trying to become."[26] Finally, he would be able to put an end to this battle and become fully himself: "He needed to build his own footbridge over the abyss and rejoin the other part of himself across space and time."[27] And, somewhat paradoxically, he would do it by splitting himself in two: by separating the "person" who was fighting—that is to say, the incomplete, "broken-down" subject—from the "man I'm trying to become"—that is, the part of the subject who was reintegrating himself into the story, so that the two would be able to meet.

It would be the meeting between the sleeping pilot and the little prince that would put an end to a long voyage.

# II

# THOU ART MY BELOVED SON*

ANTOINE DE SAINT-EXUPÉRY RECEIVED from his mother what any mother who is "good enough" should give her son. And, as far as we know, the same could be said for his three sisters and his brother. To properly fulfill one's role as a parent (which should not be confused with that of a progenitor; a *progenitor* is any man or woman who has engendered a child, but a *parent* is one who has provided care to his or her child), the parent must provide the child with what we have called the three Ps of parenting: Protect the child, Provide for the child's needs, and give him Permission to become what he is.[1] Protect, Provide, Permit: Marie seems to have fulfilled this role very well. Certainly, Antoine—Tonio—would never disagree, as proven by the tone of his letters, which I've quoted extensively here. It is a real shame that we don't have access to Marie's responses, which prevents us from fully appreciating the quality of their exchanges. Be that as it may, reading only Antoine's side is to witness a long declaration of unrestrained love, with an intensity and tonality that at times leave us feeling some discomfort, for the words we're reading could be those of a man in love

---

* "Thou art my beloved Son; with thee I am well pleased"—Luke 3:22.

addressing his beloved. But let's not see Oedipus everywhere we look: psychoanalysis outside the context of treatment is neither relevant nor of interest, while it is both in its rightful domain. Saint-Ex loved his mother and never reproached her for anything, except for—rarely—sending his money order late.

MARIE DE SAINT-EXUPÉRY WAS truly a "modern" mother, especially regarding the educational principles that were in vogue in France at the very beginning of the twentieth century. Despite her own difficulties—belonging to the aristocracy did not guarantee financial comfort, and this was particularly true in her case—she responded to her children's needs in such a way that they were not deprived. They lacked for nothing, even if their lifestyle may have seemed modest compared to that of other families of their rank. Marie protected her children. She protected them from the dangers of the world; she protected them by the example of her integrity, passing on to them her own clear and confident moral standards, but not in a coercive way; she protected them by always being available, granting them priority over anything else—although she was widowed at the age of twenty-nine, she would never "restart" her life; and she protected them through her unconditional love. Time and again, Tonio would acknowledge his gratitude to her. Thanks to her refusal to be influenced by the strict advice doled out by uncles who seemed to confuse education with training, the children lived a life of liberty in the park of Saint-Maurice-de-Rémens. One could call the time at Saint-Maurice "blessed," and it was held sacred in the writings of Marie and Simone. In fact, one of Saint-Ex's biographers saw in it a "strange echo of the books of the Countess of Ségur! Same 'good children,' same 'good little devil,' same 'model children,' a simple and modest life at a château, a diligently Christian life, sympathetic relationships with the domestic staff . . ."[2]

But Marie—and this is why she was quite modern—succeeded in what is probably the most difficult thing to succeed in for any parent: giving her children the permission to follow their own paths and not the ones she might have laid out for them, thus allowing them to become who they were and not who she might have wanted them to be. She acted, although certainly without knowing it, just as the Russian anarchist Mikhail Bakunin recommended: "Children belong nor to their parents nor to society. They belong to themselves and to their own future liberty."[3] Antoine's life was a perfect example of this. We do not know if Marie had particular plans for him, but we do know that over the years, he changed his own innumerable times, and that she never opposed him, even if we perhaps might doubt that she had ever wished to see him become a pilot. One can assume that she suffered from Antoine being so far away when he left for Africa, followed by Argentina, and that she lived in a state of constant worry, despite the reassuring words he sent her regularly, for she was familiar with the very real dangers of his profession. However, she never reproached him and she never attempted any emotional blackmail. She accepted that he was living the life that he had chosen.

Saint-Exupéry thus lived a happy childhood. Apparently. His whole life, he would remain nostalgic for it, evoking it endlessly, not as a sweet and calming memory but as a lost paradise that he despaired at not being able to inhabit still. It was as though, having left this childhood, he never managed really to begin living his life and remained instead in a hopeless state of mourning. "I'm not quite sure that I've lived since childhood," he wrote to his mother from Buenos Aires at the age of thirty.[4] For him, childhood didn't seem like part of the past but instead an inaccessible part of the present, a place of origin and an original reality rather than a memory. "Childhood, this great land that everyone leaves! Where am I from? I am from my childhood. I am from my childhood, just as one is from a country."[5] And so, because this period of childhood remained part of his reality, it wasn't integrated in the succession of days inscribed in temporality that would have transformed past into memory, one moment after the other. Saint-Ex's childhood resisted this transmutation. In order for us to understand psychologically a period of time we've lived through, it must have a completed form, a "good form" as Gestalt theory refers to it.[6] There must be harmony among the elements of a system for us to be able to perceive or conceive concisely and clearly, and this good form is indispensable for its integration in the psyche. And yet, when an element is lacking, this good form is impossible to achieve, for harmony requires completeness. What then was Saint-Exupéry's childhood missing? A father.

WE'VE CONSIDERED THE BRUTAL loss of this father several times already: he most likely died as a result of a stroke in a little train station in Var. This death is striking because of its brutality, and because it was unforeseen, at least as far as we know. Saint-Ex seems to have believed that his father had been suffering from syphilis,[7] but no one knows where he got this idea, for which there is no evidence. All the same, he regularly underwent Bordet-Wassermann tests; and since he was convinced—wrongly—that the illness was hereditary, he may have confided in a woman friend that he would have liked to have a child with a woman from the desert, for he wouldn't fear infecting her, as syphilis was already widespread throughout the region.[8] In fact, in the tertiary stage* of its development, syphilis can cause brain damage, sometimes bringing about particularly serious psychological disorders as well as strokes. At the time when Antoine's parents met, syphilis was widespread—it accounted for 15 percent of the general mortality rate—and it was certain that in the absence of any effective treatment, it generally developed into this tertiary stage, with a fatal outcome. We know that Guy de Maupassant, among many others, was a victim.[9] When Jean de Saint-Exupéry met Marie de Fonscolombe, who was twelve years younger, he was thirty-three years old. Taking into account the sexual mores at the time of "high society" youth, who frequently sowed their wild oats in brothels, it would not be implausible for him to have already contracted syphilis. As this illness is mostly transmitted during the primary stage and less frequently during the secondary stage, which can last two or three years, he could—if his infection had taken place in the prime of his youth—have had relations with his wife without her becoming infected. This hypothesis is valid not only because the circumstances of his father's death match up with it, but also and especially because the "blackout" surrounding his disappearance is astonishing. Of course, Jean de Saint-Exupéry physically disappeared from Antoine's life when the latter was not yet four years old, so it is understandable that he would hardly be mentioned by the family or biographers—he was not

---

* The primary stage is usually distinguished by the appearance of a chancre and the swelling of lymph nodes; the secondary stage, which can last for three or four years, by skin infections; and the tertiary stage, which can appear fifteen years after the initial infection, consists of cardiovascular, nervous system, and joint symptoms, and in the absence of treatment leads to death.

able to play a significant role in his son's life. But all the same . . . Simone, his daughter, mentions him twice in her memoir, and the two main biographers of Saint-Ex, Curtis Cate and Stacy de La Bruyère, mention him respectively four and three times in works of more than four hundred pages. That is not very much.

Still more perplexing is the silence surrounding his disappearance, the catastrophic consequences of his death for the family, and the void that he left, a material void as much as it was psychological and emotional. It seems that only Alain Vircondelet, in his book *Antoine de Saint-Exupéry, histoires d'une vie* (*Antoine de Saint-Exupéry: Stories From a Life*), devotes a brief chapter at the beginning to the "missing father." "This lack (of a father) no doubt contributed to the feeling of exile that would remain with him always, and to the feeling that he was in a precarious financial state, a start of constant instability. He would react by living a bohemian, often whimsical lifestyle, as though to defy destiny. . . . The fatal shadow of his father passed into his apparently happy childhood."[10] If this quite plausible hypothesis is correct—which in all likelihood we will never know—it would help us better understand his family's silence. As was the case with AIDS at the beginning of the epidemic, syphilis was considered to be a shameful disease because it was linked to sexuality, a subject that was taboo by its nature but even more so in society of the end of the nineteenth century and especially among the Catholic aristocracy.

Whether Jean de Saint-Exupéry died as a result of syphilis or from a "banal" stroke would not be worth discussing, if it weren't for our suspicion that Antoine's belief had an impact on his life, his work, and, notably, on the appearance of the little prince. Historical speculations are hardly of interest: wondering what might have happened with Saint-Ex if his father had lived is certainly futile, although we can be sure that his life would have been profoundly different. Although he belonged to a family of high nobility that could trace its roots back to the Crusades, including distinguished academics and military men—one of his great-great-grandfathers had fought in America with Lafayette—Jean de Saint-Exupéry, an inspector in an insurance company, did not appear to demonstrate remarkable qualities that might have made him a role model for his son after his death. On the other hand, to the degree that Saint-Ex was convinced, rightly or wrongly, that his father had been afflicted by a shameful disease, the symbolic place of the father took a nasty hit!

We know that, from his arrival in Paris for his studies, Antoine quite precociously took a sustained interest in "*mignonnes*," as he called them: "easy girls" who were essentially prostitutes. His first foray into literature, a short story called "Manon, danseuse"[11] ("Manon, Dancer"), is about the life of a "poor girl" who had been forced into prostitution to survive. Around the same time, he wrote to his girlfriend Renée de Saussine, who was known as Rinette, "Last night I chatted with a poor hooker. She told me . . . 'My husband just left me for a kid. . . . So I'm working the streets, or I'm trying . . . But I'm not managing very well . . . So I'm going to go "in-house" again, because I don't know how to solicit men, and I can't do it anymore. There they can pick me if they want me."[12] Obviously, the world of prostitution was not unfamiliar to him, and his attentive mother had probably warned him about the sanitary dangers that threatened young people. Perhaps it was on this occasion that she told him about the misfortune that had befallen his father, in order to be more persuasive. From then on, Saint-Ex could no longer be that father's son. Not only was his father physically absent and never portrayed as a role model, but the memory trace he left behind was shapeless and threatening: it was the fear of the transmission of a disease. And when Saint-Ex referred to God the Father whom he wanted to meet after climbing a difficult mountain, he found, as we have already noted, nothing but a chilling stone: "But on the summit of the mountain, I discovered only a heavy block of black granite—which was God."

The phrase "Thou art my beloved Son" never entirely resonated with Saint-Ex—whether he could not or would not feel it—even though it was inscribed in his own history. Among the Scripture-inspired stories that his mother told him when he was dragging his little chair around to listen to her, it seems that Antoine appreciated in particular the parable of the prodigal son.[13] How it must have spoken to him, and with what force: "But while he was yet at a distance, his father saw him and had compassion, and ran and embraced him and kissed him. . . . The father said to his servants. . . . Bring the fatted calf and kill it, and let us eat and make merry; for this my son was dead, and is alive again; he was lost, and is found" (Luke 15:19–23). One can imagine how this story of a reunion between a father and a son would have moved a little boy deprived of a father.

In sum, although his mother was perfect in both image and reality, his father didn't exist, and in his symbolic place was nothing but a boulder of black granite. A father who is absent physically, whether living away from home or deceased, can exist as an internalized paternal image that a child might use to support the construction of his psyche—but a sufficient and adequate childhood cannot be constructed without a symbolic father. In order for there to be a father in Saint-Exupéry's life, he would need to become one himself, and in that way reinvent his childhood and turn it into a memory—a nostalgic one, to be sure, but nonetheless a memory that could be integrated into his life and unified. The alternative was for it to become a lost reality that he would desperately seek to relive throughout a long, hopeless period of mourning.

Beginning with *Southern Mail*, he glimpsed the unbearableness of his condition and the path to salvation: "I was young, as though perched on some star where life would begin anew."[14] Fifteen years later, he would find a way to respond. "Once upon a time, there was a little prince who lived on a planet hardly bigger than himself, and who needed a friend. . . ."[15] He would become a father by giving birth to *The Little Prince*.

# 12

# *ELI, ELI, LEMA SABACHTANI**

No PATERNAL FIGURE WOULD emerge to compensate for his father's absence, and Saint-Exupéry lived his childhood in a world of women: mother, sisters, aunts, and governesses. Certainly, later on, he would cross paths with men who had the potential to fill this role: the "fathers" at his schools in Lyon, Le Mans, and Fribourg; Antoine Wahl, his German professor in Fribourg; Abbot Sudour in Bossuet when he was preparing for the École Navale; André Gide, who assisted him in his literary debuts; Didier Daurat; and Léon Werth. But as we know, the psyche is formed in the early years, and it is difficult to bridge the gaps or to make significant changes to its structure after that. The depressive tendencies that had been apparent in Saint-Ex beginning in adolescence, his insecurities, his symbiotic relationship with his mother, his compulsive

---

* "And about the ninth hour Jesus cried with a loud voice, 'Eli, Eli, lama sabachthani?' that is, 'My God, my God, why hast thou forsaken me'"? (Matthew 27:46). This is the only Aramaic phrase in the Gospels. It was spoken by Jesus, after he was crucified and right before his death, and is a reprisal of a quotation from Psalm 22: "My God, my God, why has thou forsaken me? Why art thou so far from helping me, from the words of my groaning?"

philandering, his addictions, and his tireless search for meaning all demonstrate that he never made up for this emptiness. He had not internalized a paternal image that was good enough, and so he remained in a way the prisoner of a threatening void. Maybe he experienced what he described in *The Wisdom of the Sands*: "That person, if he is cut off from his source, is as though divided, demolished; and he dies of asphyxiation, just as a tree does if its roots are cut."[1]

Between his deeply pious mother, the daily worship mandated by his Aunt Tricaud, the Jesuits from the Collège Notre-Dame-de-Sainte-Croix in Le Mans, and the Marianists from the Villa Saint-Jean in Fribourg, his very Christian—more precisely, very Catholic—education might have offered him a Father in the heavens, for lack of a father on Earth. But as we've seen already, this wasn't the case. Saint-Exupéry didn't "get" a religion that offered him the representation of an all-powerful anthropomorphic divinity. He himself lamented his inability to succumb to this "easy way out": "The advantage is that they look to Jesus for directions, and this is how they have faith. They will live in the monastery on medieval poetry, music, love. And nothing that you don't immerse yourself in fully will allow you to grow."[2] He acknowledged experiencing a need for the divine: "I need a childhood full of divinities. I'm crossing through such an arid land."[3] But it was less a mystical quest than it was a quest for meaning, for *the* meaning: he sought to build a lifeline. He, a mathematician and a pilot who, in a time without automatic navigational systems, had to plot out his route by tracing it on a map, knew quite well that a line can be drawn only using an x- and a y-axis. The empty place that his father had left behind meant that one of the two was missing, and so he felt lost. "I'm sad because of this strange planet on which I'm living. Because of all I don't know how to understand."[4]

However, like Bernis at Notre-Dame,[5] he didn't want to accept faith. He refused a God who could be "touched," writing: "A god that lets himself be touched is no longer a god."[6] He refused the consolation it might have provided him; this God was too closely associated with a father who was no more than a frozen void for him to want to draw near. Even if it meant wandering, he had no one but himself to find his (fore)bearings: "I understand only when I build my branches myself. . . . I just barely know when I'm there. But I never know where to go. I am quite an awkward tree."[7] These "branches" were the values by which he wanted to orient his life: friendship, duty, faithfulness to his country and to his culture, commitment that implied a willingness for self-sacrifice, sharing, compassion, responsibility toward those whom one has "tamed," contempt for that which is merely material as well as glorification of action, "doing good" instead of merely "thinking good," and the ability to experience beyond what is simply visible to the eye or comprehensible to the intelligence of reason. He would return many times to the value of confrontation: the idea that differences and divergences among people are a source of enrichment. "My friend is often the one who disagrees with me, because he is improving me."[8] Or again, in *Letter to a Hostage*: "If I differ from you, far from hurting you, I'm improving you."[9] And again in *Flight to Arras*: "In my civilization, the one who is different from me does not hurt me at all, he enriches me."[10]

These values may have directed his actions, but they did not fill, in and of themselves, the staggeringly large void left by his father's erasure. And this void, for lack of being named, referred to, or even simply looked in the face, left Saint-Ex suspended in an empty sky—a sky he nonetheless crisscrossed because it was his duty to do so, but in which he was unable find a place that would be his own. "I wonder all the time: where in the universe can I go to live that would be my home?"[11] But how could he find a home that was "his" when he had been deprived of a part of himself? This missing part could have been one of suffering; it would have been a reassuring pain because it could be spoken of, instead of a dizzying nothingness. But no one, not even Saint-Exupéry himself, designated it, named it and gave it meaning. And so the child went through his childhood without anyone seeing what he didn't know how to show, or hearing what he didn't know how to say: "And no grown-up will ever understand that this has so much importance!" [12]

In this light, the little prince's celestial odyssey could be a symbolic representation of young Antoine's own voyage, during which he met only grown-ups who didn't know how to see sheep inside their boxes. From star to star, from king to businessman, no one asks the little prince how he came to be alone on a miniscule asteroid lost in the middle of nowhere. And even when he arrives on Earth, in a desert, at first only an echo answers him, followed by a poor snake, who confesses that "one is alone among men, too." He has to wait for the aviator to hear a human voice. Through the voice of the little man to whom he had given birth, Saint-Exupéry could finally speak about his solitude, his wanderings, his abandonment, and his fruitless quest for someone to talk to. Among all the stars he visits, the little prince—just like his double, the pilot—hasn't found anyone that he can "really talk to."[13] The men he meets—and let's note that we're speaking of men in the masculine sense of the term, which is to say potential fathers—speak only of their occupations, which in these instances are without interest:

ruling for the sake of ruling, admiring themselves, drinking to forget that they drink, possessing in order to possess, lighting and extinguishing useless lights, recording the wonders of the world in dull registers. The two characters who make up Saint-Ex—the child and the aviator—land so they can find and speak with each other, or more precisely, so that the child—for he is the one who speaks, having finally decided to leave his little planet—can "wake up" the aviator. And when the two do meet, before they even know each other or know who the other is, they already agree to make a sheep appear!

Thus, as he was preparing to meet the solitary child who been wandering the skies, regarded by no one, Saint-Exupéry was careful to have at the ready an animal whose symbolic role is of signal importance in Judeo-Christianity, as he well knew. These three figures—the father, the son, and the *lamb*—together constitute a paradigmatic bedrock for Judaism as well as for Christianity.

"And Isaac said to his father Abraham, 'My father!' And he said, 'Here am I, my son.' He said, 'Behold, the fire and the wood; but where is the lamb for a burnt offering?'" (Genesis 22:7). Here Isaac, the son, is worried—for good reason—about the absence of a lamb who is supposed to be sacrificed to please the Eternal Father, God, who has in actuality demanded that the earthly father sacrifice his own son to him: "After these things God tested Abraham, and said to him, 'Abraham!' And he said, 'Here am I.' He said, 'Take your son, your only son Isaac, whom you love, and go to the land of Moriah, and offer him there as a burnt offering upon one of the mountains of which I shall tell you'" (Genesis 22:1–2). Later in the Biblical story, the Eternal Father directs Moses to order every Jewish family to sacrifice a lamb, whose blood spread on the door of the house would signal to the Angel of Death that the house should be spared from the massacre of firstborns, which should strike only Egyptians: "On the tenth day of this month they shall take every man a lamb according to their fathers' houses, a lamb for a household" (Exodus 12:3). The tradition persists of eating lamb in celebration of Passover, which commemorates the Jews' escape from Egypt. As for Christianity, it's Jesus himself who was assimilated with the sacrificial lamb: "The next day he saw Jesus coming toward him, and said, 'Behold, the Lamb of God, who takes away the sin of the world!'" (John 1:29). Jesus was designated the Son, the only son of God, whose sacrifice would save mankind. For Easter, which is to say for the celebration of the resurrection of Jesus after his crucifixion, Christians eat lamb, following the example of the Jews. The Torah, like the Gospel, teaches that the son—assimilated to or replaced by a sheep—redeems in God's eyes the mistakes of all the fathers descended from the first father, Adam, who was kneaded from clay by God's own hand.

There has been an infinite number of exegeses on the meaning of the relationships between these three figures. Let's just note that Saint-Exupéry evoked the figures—and it scarcely matters whether or not he did so consciously. The fact remains that when the child appears and is going to (re)enter the man's story, thus uniting the two figures and suggesting the symbolic father, a lamb must be present in order, through its sacrifice, to redeem the sins of the world and therefore the sins of the father. The lamb brought forth for this purpose allows for the sins of history to be wiped clean. And the child who is born, the man-in-progress, is pure and stainless: he can finally be welcomed without fear.

And so, because he was asked to write a story for children, Saint-Exupéry could give voice to this little man, who up until then had been wandering on random pages where he had made him appear. And because the child, endowed with the Word, now lived, the sleeping aviator Saint-Ex was allowed to become entirely who he was. "Now childhood has become sweet. Not only childhood, but all of my past life. I see it in perspective, like a countryside . . . and it seems to me like I am one with myself."[14] To the extent that he didn't believe in the God of his ancestors, the God whose name he did not want and was not able to pronounce, he was forbidden from entering the Holy of Holies to groan his suffering at having been abandoned. So he would never say, "My God, my God, why have you forsaken me?" like the crucified Son—but all of his works say it, all nourished by the quest for the divine that would repair his broken childhood.

In his notes to the original French edition of *The Wisdom of the Sands*, Michel Quesnel writes, "All of Saint-Exupéry's paths lead to the same point, to this God, whose presence fascinated him."[15] That is the tree whose roots he wanted to reach into the masterpiece that he never finished completing, and that he knew he would never finish. "I feel threatened, vulnerable, pressed for time, I want to finish my tree. Guillaumet is dead, I want to finish my tree quickly. I want to become something other than myself quickly. I'm no longer interested in myself. . . . I want to be something other than this when it's time to die."[16] He would never finish *The Wisdom of the Sands*, but perhaps without his ever having realized it, *The Little Prince*—that long child's prayer—had already said it all.

# 13

# DRAW ME A SHEEP . . .

THE MAGIC OF *THE Little Prince* that explains its universal success is to be found—to paraphrase the text—not in reading with the eyes but with the heart. And to be more exact, rather than "read" we should say "contemplate," "look at," or "immerse oneself in," for *The Little Prince* is reminiscent of a Wagnerian opera: it is a totality whose text is completely indissociable from its images.

What would remain of *The Little Prince* without the author's drawings?

What would these drawings represent without the story that they express?

Like the ideas expressed in the book, Saint-Ex's images can be understood as an ethical argument and had long been present in earlier writings. When he made the decision to publish a story for children, Saint-Ex felt right away that there was a necessary link between the text and *his* drawings. At one point, there was a possibility that the book might be illustrated by the painter Bernard Lamotte, but very quickly Antoine understood the necessity of doing the illustrations himself. As the manuscript shows, he viewed them as having the utmost importance and wanted to be the one to arrange the text and the images. Thus, in a letter to his editor, he explained the layout he intended very precisely: "I want absolutely, before any work is undertaken, to decide myself: a) the placement of the drawings, b) their relative size, c) the choice of which ones to print in color, d) the text to place next to the drawings. When I write for example: 'Here is the most handsome drawing that I managed to make of him . . . ,' I know perfectly well which drawing I would like to put there, whether I want it big or small, in black-and-white or in color, combined with the text or distinct."[1] It seems the relationship between the text and the images held a significance for him that went far beyond the desire to produce an original book, a "beautiful book."

THE LITTLE PRINCE OPENS with a drawing: that of a boa constrictor swallowing a wild animal, which, the narrator tells us, is a copy of an image that he had seen when he was six years old in a book about the primeval forest. This leads him to tell us that that illustration had given him the desire to draw, and he presents us with his "Drawing Number One," a boa constrictor digesting an elephant, in which the grown-ups had seen only a hat. Realizing that they always needed explanation, he then drew his "Drawing Number Two," in which you can see an elephant inside the boa constrictor; but despite this pedagogical effort, he was advised to leave aside his drawings and devote himself instead to geography, history, arithmetic, and grammar. And so, discouraged by the failure of his two first drawings, he abandoned at the age of six a "magnificent career as a painter."

But oddly enough, when the little prince appears, he awakens the sleeping aviator by asking him, "Please . . . draw me a sheep!" and he repeats this request three times in a row. In fact, the first three utterances by the little prince consist in nothing but this simple and rather incongruous request, to draw a sheep for him. Their initial meeting is thus doubly surprising: where did this little man come from, in the middle of the desert; who is he; and why is he addressing a pilot, who is himself lost amid the sands, stubbornly demanding that he draw a sheep? Incidentally, the phrase "Draw me a sheep" quickly became emblematic, a sort of metonym used to refer to the work as a whole. Somewhat surprisingly, before even responding, the narrator presents a portrait for us of a "most extraordinary little person," whom we knew until then only by his "funny little voice." This portrait is not a written description, but rather a drawing: "Here is the best portrait that, later, I was able to make of him." And the aviator feels the need to return immediately to what he had told us on the preceding page: that his career as a painter had been thwarted by the blindness of grown-ups. It is only after this insistent reminder that his meeting and his conversation with the little man really take place.

The little prince first makes contact with the narrator by uttering this request, which brings the narrator back to when he was six years old. It is as though the request frees him from an interdiction around which his life had been constructed. He had been told to stop drawing because it wasn't a serious thing to do, so he had become serious, or at least he had tried. He realized, when he was among grown-ups, that they stubbornly saw only a hat instead of a boa constrictor digesting an elephant, so he spoke to them about bridge, golf, politics, and neckties, which allowed him to pass as a sensible man. But the cost of this adaptation was significant, for, as he tells us, "I lived alone, without anyone I could truly talk to." Up until the little prince's appearance, it appears that the narrator had lived by himself, forcing himself to be understood by grown-ups and not to speak truthfully—that is to say, to speak falsely, adopting what the English psychoanalyst David Winnicott defined as a "false self," meaning unlike one's real self.\*

The little man's demand thus disrupted the aviator's life. By ordering him to draw, he shattered the protective shell into which the narrator had withdrawn as a response to the grown-ups' expectations. He took away the narrator's mask, confronting him with the little boy of six who had dreamed of finding a common language with adults, who naively had believed that even serious people could see beyond the reality visible to their eyes and knew the secret that the fox had unveiled to the little prince: "One can see well only with the heart. What is essential is invisible to the eye."

No one doubts that the aviator who narrates this extraordinary meeting is Antoine de Saint-Exupéry himself. When Flaubert claimed, "Madame Bovary, c'est moi!" ("I am Madame Bovary!"), he was only reminding us of the writer's work in projecting his own motivations, desires, worries, and way of thinking on to his characters; clearly, Flaubert was not actually Madame Bovary. But it's different for the aviator whose plane had broken down in the desert. Saint-Exupéry was an aviator himself, and he often needed to land his aircraft in the sand without knowing for certain whether he'd be able to take off again. Surely, then, the author placed himself in the middle of the action of *The Little*

---

\* Donald Woods Winnicott (1896–1971) was an English pediatrician, psychiatrist, and psychoanalyst. When the development of a child's "space for play and creativity" is restricted too early or even forbidden entirely, the child's ability to adapt to his environment is compromised. To survive, the self dissociates into its false self. This false self is dependent on the mother's needs and subconscious psychological difficulties.

*Prince*, imagining a wonderful story stemming from his own personal history, not a novelized version of it.

Given this, one might wonder why the drawings are so important in this tale—far from being simple illustrations, they're inseparable from the written narrative, part of the work's very essence and expressing as much as the words do. One might also question the insistence with which the narrator explains and remembers the grown-ups' order to "leave aside" his drawings, to which he attributes his obligation to abandon his career as a painter at the age of six and to make another choice for his life: "So I had to choose another profession, and I learned to pilot airplanes." Thus the man who may have become an aviator simply by default was awakened by a voice asking him to draw, as if it was fitting that he return to the point of departure and rediscover his six-year-old self, who still dreamed of drawing. Let's note as well the exact way the narrator tells us when the story he is about to recount took place: "So I lived alone, without anyone I could truly talk to, until my plane broke down in the Sahara Desert six years ago."[2] Exactly six years before writing *The Little Prince*, Saint-Exupéry had the aforementioned accident in the desert, not the Sahara but in Libya, where he had a very close brush with death. Six years later he writes this in the book: "'Ah!' I said to the little prince. 'Your memories are lovely, but I haven't repaired my plane yet, I have nothing left to drink, and I too would be very happy if I could walk leisurely toward a spring!' 'My friend, the fox . . . ' he said to me. 'My dear little man, this no longer has anything to do with the fox!' 'Why not?' 'Because we're going to die of thirst.'"[3] Reading this, can there be any doubt that when Saint-Ex was writing *The Little Prince* he was re-immersing himself explicitly in his memories of a time when he thought he was going to lose his life?

It may have been a Bedouin, coming out of nowhere, who brought the real Saint-Ex back to life ("With one movement of his torso and a sweeping glance, he had created life, and so he seemed to me like a god. . . . It was a miracle . . . he was walking on the sand toward us, like a god on the sea"[4]), but in the tale it's the little prince's request that allows the aviator to begin to "truly" live, for he erases the aviator's years of solitude and distraction by commanding him to draw a sheep. In order to draw, the aviator is obliged to see, to look. Shortly before beginning to write this story, Saint-Ex had written, "And so I seem to have come to the end of a long pilgrimage. I have discovered nothing, but as though waking from sleep, I simply see again what I was no longer looking at."[5]

THIS REFERENCE TO THE six years that had passed between the accident and the writing of *The Little Prince* does not enlighten us about the other six years, however—between the aviator's birth and the moment when he was discouraged from becoming a talented painter. We do know, though, that at that age Saint-Ex was confronted with a traumatic event: his father's death. Could that tragedy have led him more or less consciously to pinpoint that moment as the one when he renounced the particular magic of childhood that the little prince would bring back to life?

As mentioned before, we have very little information about Antoine de Saint-Exupéry's childhood at our disposal. He himself practically never mentioned it, other than the occasional allusion, mostly in the form of reminiscences provoked by certain situations that reminded him of memories, images, or smells, like Proust savoring his famous madeleine. How did he react to the tragedy that turned his family life upside down? For even if it's likely that, thanks to his very young age, he had no conscious memory of the event, there's no doubt that his psyche was affected by the grief and that it retained subconscious traces of the memory.

In any case, nothing suggests that he was ever actually prevented from drawing. To tell the truth, nothing suggests that he was ever passionate about drawing, unlike with mechanics and gardening; the latter appears to have been an abandoned vocation, but no doubt an authentic one, for in one of his last letters he wrote, "I was made to be a gardener."[6] The prohibition that the aviator in *The Little Prince* complains of, and on which he bases his bitter critique of grown-ups who "never understand anything by themselves," is therefore not a reference to something that actually occurred in Saint-Exupéry's childhood. It is instead a metaphor substituting, consciously or not, for some other prohibition, whether explicitly stated or simply experienced, that imposed on him or forbade a way of doing, feeling, thinking, or being. This prohibition must have been so significant and destructive that, until he could be liberated from it by a little prince asking him to draw, he "lived alone, without anyone he could truly talk to."

Drawing seems therefore to represent the forbidden—that which he had to renounce in a repudiation that was so oppressive it didn't allow him to be himself, to become what he really was, or to live his true life.

# 14

# THE ANNUNCIATION

"IN THE SIXTH MONTH the angel Gabriel was sent from God to a city of Galilee named Nazareth, to a virgin betrothed to a man whose name was Joseph, of the house of David; and the virgin's name was Mary. And he came to her and said, 'Hail, O favored one, the Lord is with you!' But she was greatly troubled at the saying, and considered in her mind what sort of greeting this might be. And the angel said to her, 'Do not be afraid, Mary, for you have found favor with God. And behold, you will conceive in your womb and bear a son, and you shall call his name Jesus" (Luke 1:26–31). This is how the Evangelist tells us of the angel Gabriel's announcement to Mary that she will bear a child. His words are shocking to the young girl: "And Mary said to the angel, 'How can this be, since I have no husband?'" (Luke 1:34). But the child who is to be born will not be a normal child: "The Holy Spirit will come upon you, and the power of the Most High will overshadow you; therefore the child to be born will be called holy, the Son of God" (Luke 1:35).

Viewing this text through a literary and not a theological lens, this story tells us that a child will be born who is part of God's very essence. As the Son of God, he is, according to Christian doctrine, an integral part of the divinity, along with the Holy Spirit: he will be truly man and truly God, the incarnation of God, the Word incarnated. It's the foundation of Christianity, which aimed to promote a new alliance. The evangelical message was intended to put an end to the Torah and to Mosaic Law, and the incarnation of God in a child established the latter as a new origin. Up until then, the child was the son of man; henceforth, man becomes the son of the child. And the Creator would invite humankind to embark on the same path as he did if they wanted to reach truth: "Unless you turn and become like children, you will never enter the kingdom of heaven" (Matthew 18:3). The route thus laid out passes through a return to childhood: to qualify for entrance into the Kingdom of Heaven—that is to say, to become oneself—one must have lived through childhood and have retained the ability to identify with it, to meet the child that one once was.[1]

Now that we've refreshed our memory about the evangelical teachings by which Saint-Ex was raised, let's return to the meeting between the aviator and the little prince. At first, the aviator doesn't see the little prince; rather, it's his voice that awakens him. "The first night, I went to sleep on the sand. . . . So you can imagine my astonishment when, at sunrise, I was awakened by a funny little voice. It said, 'Please . . . draw me a sheep!' 'What?!' 'Draw me a sheep. . . .' I jumped to my feet as though I'd been struck by lightning. I rubbed my eyes hard. I looked all around. And I saw a most extraordinary little man, who was looking at me with great seriousness."[2]

In his notes on the text, Michel Autrand points out, "As for Joan of Arc, the voice comes first."[3] This reference to the sacred—isolated, as it is—might appear out of place in a text of literary analysis unless it's intended to convey the perception of a religious atmosphere that saturates the story, perhaps even without the author's knowledge. Until this moment, the aviator's storytelling is, dare we say, completely down-to-earth and somewhat banal. He has told us, not without humor, about a child's disappointment after having been discouraged by grown-ups who were as sensible as they were barely perceptive. But everything changes radically with this voice that emerges from the desert and wakes the sleeping man. Nothing indicates that Saint-Ex had episodes of the Bible in mind when he imagined this situation; were the echoes subconscious, then? To our knowledge, he never spoke of them, but how can we not take note of these odd similarities?

The Gospel of Mark opens with a quotation from the prophet Isaiah (40:3): "The voice of one crying in the wilderness: Prepare the way of the Lord, make his paths straight" (Mark 1:3), a quotation repeated by three other evangelists (Matthew 3:3, Luke 3:4, John 1:23). All four borrow from the Old Testament prophet in order to announce the arrival of a child who will be the "beloved Son" of God, the Messiah for whom the Jews have been waiting for generations. In *The Little Prince*, there's also a voice in the desert—a child's voice—that awakens the man.

The narrator doesn't describe this "completely extraordinary" child to us; instead, he draws a portrait of him, one that is "much less astonishing than its model." He draws him for the first and only time in all of his majesty, clothed in a ceremonial coat, boots, and holding a sword. It's hard to believe that he would be dressed in this way, since this outfit seems most incompatible with traveling in the sand; in all the other drawings, he's dressed in a very ordinary way, with the exception of a scarf (which, to tell the truth, seems poorly adapted to the climate of the Sahara). But the aviator wants us to understand right away that this little man is a little prince, a title that won't be revealed to us until the end of the second chapter when he says, "And that is how I made the acquaintance of the little prince," without telling us what kind of prince he was. At least, we do know that, in principle, a prince is the son of a king.

Their meeting, then, is at first only a voice and words: "Draw me a sheep." Only then does the funny little man materialize. The beginning of the Gospel of John says, "In the beginning was the Word, and the Word was with God, and the Word was God. . . . And the Word became flesh and dwelt among us, full of grace and truth; we have beheld his glory, glory as of the only Son from the Father" (John 1:1, 1:14). The aviator heard the voice speak its liberating demand, and then as though "struck by lightning," according to his own words, he was looking at a little prince in all of his glory.

But whose son is the little prince? Or which Son is he intended to signify?

He appears out of nowhere at sunrise, and the aviator speaks of an "apparition"; he is instantly enthralled by this child, who looks at him "with great seriousness." "When a mystery is too awe-inspiring, one dare not disobey," and this submissiveness in the face of a mystery is reminiscent of Mary's to the angel: "And Mary said, 'Behold, I am the handmaid of the Lord; let it be to me according to your word'" (Luke 1:38). Does not this little prince, fallen from the sky, share similar traits with an angel? Traditionally, in Christian iconography, angels look like pretty children with golden hair, precisely like the little prince—who, when he appeared in Saint-Ex's earlier drawings, also happened to be outfitted with wings.[4]

Thus, to begin this first meeting between a man and a child, Saint-Ex offers us a scene borrowed from the Bible. There is the setting: an immense and empty desert of sand. There are the characters: a sleeping man, whose image we never see, on his own and under threat of death; and a mysterious, grave child, who first speaks in order to express a request and then appears, at which point the man awakens with a start as though "struck by lightning" (and lightning is frequently evoked as a manifestation of the All-Powerful). There is the evocation of an animal that is omnipresent in Biblical writings: a sheep. And, later on, another that is an omen of death in both the Torah and the tale: the snake. And this Biblical scene, this apparition that is supernatural in the real sense of the word, opens with an ending: a break in the man's life that will mark a sort of rebirth.

Everything that came before this moment, in the first chapter, was about a prohibition, an unsatisfied desire, as we've already noted: to become a painter, to draw and be understood, accepted as he was, by the grown-ups. The lack of this understanding left the man trapped in solitude, for he had no one he could talk to. In the Bible, we come across similar situations several times, in which people who have been prevented from acting or being are liberated in a flash, and are thus able to become fulfilled. This can be found as early as in the Book of Genesis in the Torah. Abram and Sarai (who would soon become Abraham and Sarah, but we will return to that), who were quite advanced in age, were not able to have a child together. Then an extraordinary event turned their lives upside down: God appeared to them to announce that they would have a son, whom they should name Isaac. This announcement stunned the couple to the point of hilarity:[5] "Then Abraham fell on his face and laughed, and said to himself, 'Shall a child be born to a man who is a hundred years old? Shall Sarah, who is ninety years old, bear a child?' . . . it had ceased to be with Sarah after the manner of women. So Sarah laughed to herself, saying, 'After I have grown old, and my husband is old, shall I have pleasure?'" (Genesis 17:17, 18:11–12). And so Sarai became Sarah, meaning that her name no longer meant "my princess" (the princess of her father who called her this) but rather simply "princess," a name freed from the generational shackles. After this announcement, she would be able to give birth.

We come across similar episodes in the New Testament, not only with Mary, as previously mentioned, but also her kinswoman, Elizabeth: "[Zechariah and Elizabeth] had no child, because Elizabeth was barren, and both were advanced in years. . . . And there appeared to him an angel of the Lord. . . . Zechariah was troubled when he saw him, and fear fell upon him. But the angel said to him, 'Do not be afraid, Zechariah, for your prayer is heard, and your wife Elizabeth will bear you a son, and you shall call his name John" (Luke 1:7–13). In these stories, we are told that these women—because they are too old, or infertile, or don't have any husbands—could not have children, could not bring new life into the world, could not keep their bloodlines alive. Only a divine annunciation can lift the prohibition. A messenger appears and speaks, liberating them immediately and allowing them finally to become fulfilled.

Likewise, is it not a liberation—the lifting of the prohibition on drawing—that the little prince announces? He is himself a child, but he is a serious one: watchful, dreamy, contemplative, who asks many questions even though he rarely responds to any asked of him, and who—unlike grown-ups, who "never understand anything by themselves"—understands everything right away, including that the first picture the aviator draws for him is not a hat but rather a boa constrictor with an elephant inside. This little prince, who "looked at [the aviator] quite seriously," who "repeated himself very slowly, as if he were speaking of something very serious," who "smiled gently and indulgently," who sank into a "meditative silence," who "remarks seriously," appears to be a "completely extraordinary little man," the bearer of wisdom that is rarely observed in children (although without a doubt, this is due to our own lack of attention). But must not he have been filled with wisdom in order to appear like a divine messenger, come to relieve a heavy burden from the aviator with a broken plane in the desert?

THE HYPOTHESIS OF A divine, or perhaps Christ-like, dimension to the little prince is further supported by Saint-Ex's essential choice in how to end the story: with the little prince's disappearance and apparent death. This ending was not originally to the taste of Saint-Ex's New York editors, which is understandable if the tale was considered to be a "real" fairy tale, intended for children. But looking closer, it doesn't appear that the little prince truly dies. He himself warned the aviator, "I will look as though I'm in pain. I will look a little as though I am dying. It is like that. Do not come to see that, it's not worth the trouble. . . ." and later, "I will look as though I'm dead, and that will not be true." The circumstances of the little prince's death give the event the feeling of an unreal lightness: "There was nothing but a flash of yellow next to his ankle. He remained motionless for a moment. He did not scream. He fell gently, like a tree falls. It did not even make any sound, because of the sand."

We understand that the snake, that "coil the color of the moonlight," has kept his promise. He was the first to speak to the little prince upon his arrival on Earth, telling him, "'I can carry you farther than a ship.' . . . 'Whomever I touch, I send back to the ground he came from' . . . 'You fill me with pity, you who are so weak on this granite Earth. I can help you some day if you miss your planet too much. I can . . .' 'Oh! I understand quite well,' said the little prince, 'but why do you always speak in riddles?' 'I solve them all,' said the snake." The Biblical tone should be noted here: God says to Adam, "In the sweat of your face you shall eat bread till you return to the ground, for out of it you were taken; you are dust, and to dust you shall return" (Genesis 3:19). Recall also that this death sentence was the result of a snake's tempting words, and that these are almost word-for-word the same as those of the snake in the tale who offers his services to the little prince. And what's more: Jesus had just been delivering a sermon to a crowd, telling the story of a sower sowing seeds, of which some had fallen by the wayside and been eaten by birds, some had fallen into stony ground and were burned by the sun, and some were choked by thorns. Only the seed that fell into good soil was able to bear fruit. "Then the disciples came and said to him, 'Why do you speak to them in parables?'" (Matthew 13:10). A parable is a sort of riddle, is it not? Speaking in parables means to speak indirectly, obscurely—and doesn't the little prince ask the snake why he always speaks in riddles?

Likewise, if we listen to the little prince's last words, "There . . . that is all," aren't they similar to the last words of the crucified Jesus, "It is finished" (John 19:30)? Then, when the aviator tells us about the little prince's "death" six years afterward, he explains, "Now I am somewhat consoled. That is to say . . . not entirely. But I know quite well that he returned to his planet, for, at sunrise, I didn't find his body." He saw the child get bitten by the snake and fall onto the sand, but the next day the body had disappeared: again, how can we not notice a reference to Christ's "death"? In his notes on the text, Michel Autrand is correct when he writes, "In a completely secular context, such a disappearance reminds us of the end of Jesus's earthly life."[6] The day after the Sabbath, "very early . . . when the sun had risen" (Mark 16:2), Mary Magdalene, Mary the mother of James, and Salome, the women who had come with Jesus from Galilee, went to the tomb carrying spices to anoint his body and "found the stone rolled away from the tomb, but when they went in, they did not find the body" (Luke 24:2).

Like Christ, the little prince was "taken up into heaven" (Mark 16:19). He returned to his planet, and his body disappeared; of course, as Saint-Ex notes, "It was not a very heavy body." The aviator then draws a picture of the landscape, which is now empty: "the most beautiful and saddest landscape in the world" where the little prince "appeared on Earth, and then disappeared." And ever since, the aviator has been waiting for his return: "Don't leave me in my misery: write me quickly and tell me he has returned." The book ends with this sentence, this waiting—just as Christians wait for the Second Coming, Christ's return to glory. During the Last Supper, the last meal he took with his disciples, Jesus told them, "And when I go and prepare a place for you, I will come again and will take you to myself, that where I am you may be also" (John 14:3).

Did the wait for the Little Prince's return feel so long to the aviator that he decided, whether deliberately or subconsciously, to go find the little prince himself by launching his plane toward the stars, one sunny July morning?

# 15

# THE ASCENSION

"And after six days Jesus took with him Peter and James and John his brother, and led them up a high mountain apart. And he was transfigured before them, and his face shone like the sun, and his garments became white as light" (Matthew 17:1–2). In this well-known episode from the Gospels, Jesus unveils his real nature and tells his disciples about the ordeal that is to come for him: "But I tell you that Elijah has already come, and they did not know him, but did to him whatever they pleased. So also the Son of man will suffer at their hands" (Matthew 17:12).

The summer of 1942, when Saint-Ex began drafting *The Little Prince* in New York, was probably the worst time of his life. He was in poor health; his personal life was erratic; and he was separated from his family and friends, attacked harshly by part of the French community, faced with financial difficulties, and ignored by all the authorities to whom he had made clear his desire to fight. In fact, until the end of 1942 when the Allies landed in North Africa, there was no theater of operations in which it was possible for him to join a combat unit. Not only did his body and his life weigh heavily upon him during this period of exile, but he expected nothing good from a future that seemed to him to be destined for inevitable decline: "So

I am profoundly sad—deeply sad. I am sad for my generation, which has been emptied of anything human. . . . Nothing is left other than the phenomenon of slow or fast digestion. I hate these times with all my might. Man is dying of thirst."[1] And more: "Hatred. Everything is hatred. Poor country! . . . Grief has taken my breath away"[2]; "I cannot bear these times, I cannot. . . . Everything has gotten worse. It's dark in my head and cold in my heart"[3]; "My God, how men disgust me. . . . I swear to you that I have nothing to do here, among those people, on this planet, where I can be neither understood nor loved. I am alone, alone, alone. More alone than dead. . . . I need a childhood full of divinities. I'm crossing a land that is truly arid."[4]

It was during this period of hopelessness that the little prince made his appearance, accomplished through the miracle of the meeting between the aviator lost in the desert and this funny little man, who until then had been only a scribble that had accompanied Antoine for a long time. As for the aviator, he disappeared, erasing himself in the true sense of the term, for he was never drawn into the tale. There is a preliminary sketch showing the aviator's hand holding a hammer, which fortunately never made it into the book. The author could only be a voice. He couldn't portray his own body or face, not even his hand. He made the burdened, suffering man disappear—the wounded man loaded down with the weight of years and grief, the man who was a prisoner to his contradictory affections and unrelievable anguish, his broken relationships with those he loved, with a childhood garden he'd had to leave behind.

Then he transfigured himself. The weighty figure of the aging man gave way to the ethereal child whose golden hair shone like the sun, like a star. Saint-Ex cast off his rags. During the course of long sleepless nights, he wrote and drew, alone, surrounded by sound and fury; it was then that he incarnated himself in this solitary child, in the middle of a silent desert between the sand and the stars. He liberated himself, looked at himself, and let himself be seen as he always truly was: "I hid from [the grown-ups] the fact that I've always been five or six years old at heart."

Who was this hidden child, who was forbidden from revealing and expressing himself? How did he survive inside this adult who was trying, despite everything, to appear like a grown-up? And after this unveiling and reunification, was the ultimate goal of his life attained?

The little prince had just been born when, in May 1943, Saint-Ex was allowed to rejoin the Free French Forces of North Africa. He had achieved his goal: to rejoin his comrades in the II/33 reconnaissance group that he had been attached to in 1940. He was euphoric. Finally, he could leave the microcosm of New York, with all of its little dramas and encrusted hatred, and distance himself from the women who were dear to him but also complicated and jealous, and from his demanding editors. He could stop moving house incessantly to please Consuelo, whose hysterical crises he could no longer bear. In Manhattan, he procured an old uniform with sleeves that were too long and shoulders that were too narrow, but he was very proud of it. He did a round of goodbyes. Everyone agreed that they found him radiant, full of energy, and impatient to be in the center of the action again. On April 13, 1943, at noon, he boarded the SS *Stirling Castle*. The crossing took two weeks, and on May 4, he landed in Algiers and settled into the house of a friend, the doctor Georges Pélissier.

His euphoria was short-lived.

Although he had found his comrades again and returned to flying and contact with the enemy, he lived the day-to-day reality of military life with less enthusiasm. From Oujda, Morocco, he wrote, "This herd-like existence in the middle of an American base, these hurried, standing, ten-minute meals . . . a sort of abstract building where we are crammed in, three to a room—this terrible human desert, in a word—has nothing to warm my heart."[5] And even when he joined his squadron in Sardinia, the quotidian experience weighed on him heavily. "Of course, I love them, my brave comrades in the squadron," he wrote in July 1944. "But nonetheless I'm suffering terribly from the absence of human contact. The Spirit matters. And during all the dinners here I get the bitter impression of having wasted a tremendous amount of time. . . . And yet I silence the greater part of myself. And I miss everything."[6] And again, in a letter addressed to Pierre Dalloz, dated July 30, the evening before his disappearance: "Here, we're far from the cesspool of hatred, but despite the kindness of the squadron, it's still a little bit of human misery. I don't have anyone, ever, to talk to. It's already something to have the wherewithal to live. But what spiritual solitude."[7] It's as though, now that the little prince had left "for good," Saint-Ex once again had no one he could "really talk to." The resurrection that the little prince seemed to have occasioned was nothing but a flash in the pan, and Saint-Ex resumed his ordeal once again.

During the nine months he was forbidden to fly, which he spent largely in Algiers, Saint-Ex hit bottom. Seemingly, everything conspired to weaken him, and it was as if he was complicit in his own downfall.

First of all: politics. This was not new, but with liberation fast approaching, rivalries, renewed hatreds, and sometimes sordid ambitions ran riot in the backwater of Algeria. The ambiguity of his initial attitude toward Vichy and de Gaulle exacerbated the hostility of those who would henceforth be the sole and effective directors of the France that was at war. Tension with the Gaullists, which had so tainted his sojourn in the United States, took on an even more violent dimension in North Africa. It has to be said that Saint-Ex didn't help matters. In order to obtain the coveted authorization to fly again, he drew dangerously close to the rival Giraudists, notably René Chambe, whom he had known in Algiers in 1940 and who had been promoted to general and Giraud's minister of information. He even agreed to undertake a brief propaganda mission to show his support for Giraud in the latent conflict between him and de Gaulle about who would represent Fighting France. However, from his first meeting with Giraud, Saint-Ex lost any illusions he might have had about him, if indeed he had any, given that his choice was dictated more by aversion to the man in London than by the seductive powers of an almost caricatural military man who was obviously incapable of preventing the unstoppable rise of the political animal who was General de Gaulle. On leaving a breakfast with Giraud that Chambe had organized to introduce the two, Saint-Ex wrote, "Poor Giraud. What a jerk. And what a pack of jerks surround him. I'm leaving this meeting more disgusted than ever."[8] But this cruel private assessment in no way changed the Gaullists' aggressiveness, although it appears Saint-Ex tended to exaggerate its reach, in somewhat paranoid fashion.

It's true that nothing was done to facilitate his return to a combat unit, and he was forbidden to accompany the crew members of the *Curie*, a ship in the Free French fleet, on patrol. It's true that his works were never among the French books sent over from New York. It's true that in October, when de Gaulle gave a speech in Algiers honoring French writers who had exiled themselves in order to not be subject to the German occupation, he deliberately neglected to mention Saint-Ex, whom he also refused to receive when Saint-Ex, in desperation, tried to set up a meeting.* But the pilot was convinced that he was the victim of demonic conspiracies. "I have proof (of what I had suspected) that the Gaullists are stealing all my letters. I'm in such distress, it's as if I'm in prison. The letters addressed to me go into God-knows-which black cabinet and will never be removed again."[9] And: "Personally, I say that the wall is getting thicker. I say that the hatred all around is condensing. . . . I came here only to shut myself in a trap. I can no longer bear the defamation, or the insults, or this tremendous lack of work. . . . I feel as though I've been slowly buried. . . . I'm already up to my knees in this quicksand. It would be an unlikely miracle if I were able to extricate even my thighs. Tomorrow it will be up to my stomach. It's taking me *straight* to the dungeon."[10] Saint-Ex was wearing himself down, obsessed with this alleged conspiracy by the supporters of the one he called the "Great Mogol," whom he suspected of wanting to establish a dictatorship in France like Salazar's in Portugal after carrying out a bloody purge. He even imagined that he could be a victim of it. Speaking about

---

* De Gaulle would later regret having refused this meeting: "Several years later, when I was in Algiers, [Saint-Ex] arrived. He asked to meet with me. I thought about it. I said to myself, 'Well, I'm going to make him wait a little.' And, alas, I never saw him. . . . It caused me a lot of grief. It's as though there are two men in me, the man and the general. Sometimes, the man would gladly do something that the general cannot do, not yet, not right away" (quoted from Stacy de La Bruyère, *Saint-Exupéry*, 477).

himself, he wrote: "'We'll have to shoot him. . . . Why? . . . Because in the United States, he didn't acknowledge General de Gaulle. . . .' Really? How flattering! How proud I am of myself! Oh, men . . ."[11] He even went so far as to compare the Gaullists to the Nazis: "They're a bunch of crabs who don't know anything but hatred. . . . They've reinvented the crime of lese majesty and the law of sacrilege. Full-blown Nazism,"[12] and "I don't like the General de Gaulle any more today. He is the threat of dictatorship. He is national socialism."[13]

As the days passed, the atmosphere in Algiers became unbearable to him. "What human misery this country is! This garbage bin of the continents. This backwater, where everything is falling apart. This moldy, provincial police station. This extraordinary absurdity of the pawns who are in power. This groveling while waiting for permission to open fire."[14] Reading these letters, which were addressed to his very dear Nelly—even if we know he was seeking consolation from her in order to ease his sense of solitude and that, to that end, he wouldn't hesitate to exaggerate what he was enduring—it is troubling to note a certain psychological disorder rising to the surface of his discourse. All the more so in that, over the course of these months of forced inaction, he seemed to everyone to be utterly worn out, worried, and struggling to communicate. He isolated himself in the bathtub; he drank a lot; he was sometimes talkative and overly cheerful, sometimes silent and on the verge of tears; he absorbed himself in mathematical or linguistic problems. There were even reports of episodes of confusion, where it seemed to him he had left the company of a friend barely two or three minutes earlier, when in fact almost two hours had passed.[15] In short, a clinical picture that suggests at the very least a fairly severe depressive episode.

IT IS TRUE THAT his health hadn't improved when he left New York—far from it. He wrote his wife that he'd aged a hundred years since his arrival in Algiers. He thought he had stomach cancer; he continued to suffer from the sequelae of his old wounds; he complained of losing his hair and his teeth; and he stuffed himself with sulfonamides to stave off various infections and with alcohol to ease the pain, which caused serious gastrointestinal problems. In November, after returning very late to the home of Doctor Pélissier, where he was staying, he had a serious fall on the stairs and convinced himself, despite the results of various radiological tests, that he had fractured a vertebra. The incident resulted in a long dispute with the doctor, whom he reproached for not taking his injury seriously.

When he was finally able to fly again, although he was delighted to go back to the fight with his fellow pilots, it came at the cost of true physical and psychological suffering. He needed help putting on his flight suit and lacing up his boots— for he couldn't bend down—as well as hoisting himself up and being crammed into the cockpit, which was not intended for a man of his girth, and then extracted from it. In several poignant photos taken by John Philips a few days before his disappearance, we see him grimacing in pain as he's being helped to slip into his heavy pilot's getup. He evokes Jesus climbing up to Golgotha carrying his heavy cross, assisted by Simon of Cyrene. In the event his plane was damaged, he knew perfectly well that he'd be incapable of extracting himself from the cockpit. He needed twice as much oxygen as the others thanks to his size, and after spending six hours at high altitude without pressurization, he would return completely drained. When to these difficulties was added the complexity of the tasks to be carried out and of operating a plane like the P-38, flying held none of the intoxication it once had in the rudimentary planes he'd piloted with his face exposed to the elements. It was a difficult, tiring, and painful job for an aging man. His physical suffering was permanent, and he also suffered from a profound sense of isolation that the friendships he'd rekindled or struck up since his return to combat did not allay.

When he left America, he left behind his wife, Consuelo, who no doubt wore him down with her whims and her hysterical fits, but whom he missed nonetheless, for he had devoted himself to protecting her, considering her a small, fragile, defenseless being in a cruel world. He wrote his mother at the beginning of the war, "Maman, the more the war and dangers and threats to the future go on, the more I worry about those for whom I'm responsible. Poor little Consuelo, so weak, so abandoned, fills me with infinite pity. If she takes refuge one day in Southern France, welcome her, maman, as though she is your daughter, out of love for me."[16] He continued to want to protect her from a distance, writing to her, "Take care of yourself, watch over yourself, protect yourself, never go out in the evenings, don't catch cold."[17] Despite this compassion, he reproached her, which is at least understandable, for having moved in with Denis de Rougemont.

He no longer had any contact with his New York girlfriends, such as Silvia, Hedda, and Nathalie. Fortunately, Nelly de Vogüé remained faithful. She even visited him in Algiers in August of 1943, attracting the suspicions of the clandestine services of the United States, which was concerned about this woman's movements in a strategic sector. Saint-Ex welcomed her in a tiny and uncomfortable room—a former laundry room that Doctor Pélissier had given him to use—and forced her to read hundreds of pages of what was supposed to become his grand masterpiece. To make sure she finished the job, he had her swallow some pills of Benzedrine, an amphetamine he used to fight fatigue during his missions. She didn't hold it against him and stayed until November before returning to London. They continued a passionate correspondence, but never saw each other again.

In the meantime, he met a young nurse on a train with whom he apparently fell in love. He wrote to her often, drew for her numerous little princes, arranged dates, and pursued her with numerous telephone calls, but the young woman avoided him. This unshared passion did bring us *Lettres à l'inconnue* (which translates to "Letters to the Female Stranger," although it hasn't been published in English), a collection of love letters finally published in France in 2008, but this romantic setback only added to his despair. "There is no little prince today, nor ever again. The little prince is dead. Or rather, he has become completely skeptical. A skeptical little prince is no longer a little prince. I blame you for having destroyed him."[18] This episode, altogether fairly banal, supports the hypothesis of the dissolution of the "little prince effect" on Saint-Exupéry himself. The magical moment in which Antoine resurrected himself by reuniting with his childhood didn't last long: the little prince felt he needed to return to his rose, and Saint-Exupéry to his own thorns.

He was almost entirely without news of his family, but he learned that the Agay château, where his sister Didi lived with her husband and children, had been destroyed by the Germans in order to fortify coastal defenses. He attempted to send his mail by airdrop or through resistance movement. "I'm worried for you, my dear little old maman. How unhappy these times are. It wounded me to the core that Didi lost her house."[19]

These separations, losses, and conflicts meant that despite his much-wished-for return to a combat unit, his morale was at its lowest. The letters he sent over the course of his last months, and even his last evening—the ones that would be found on his table after he'd disappeared,[20] in which he'd written candidly about his weariness, discouragement, and resignation, even about waiting for death—all attest to this.

DID HE HAVE A premonition of death? Did he feel its call?

One might think so. In the days leading up to his last flight, he made lengthy goodbyes, decided on the future of his precious manuscripts, charged Gavoille with distributing his possessions, and told everyone repeatedly that he felt indifferent about dying. Few were surprised to hear of his disappearance, and most were expecting such an end: Hedda Sterne and Silvia Hamilton-Reinhardt were certain, when he left them in New York, that they would never see him again; Anne Lindbergh, who was distraught, admitted that she wasn't surprised, nor was Nelly de Vogüé; his agent Max Becker had felt for a long time that Saint-Ex had a close relationship with death. But on the evening of July 31, all that was known was that his plane had taken off, risen up toward the sky, and disappeared, along with its pilot.

"So then the Lord Jesus, after he had spoken to them, was taken up into heaven" (Mark 16:19).

# 16

# THE UNCOVERING*

ON JULY 31, 1944, at 3:30 p.m., Vernon Robison, the American air liaison officer in charge of the II/33 squadron, filed an interrogation report for Major Saint-Exupéry's tenth mission. The report ended with the sentence *Pilot did not return and is presumed lost.*

The "Millennial Reich" was facing inevitable and imminent collapse. The Allied troops were advancing on Paris from the beaches of Normandy, Rome had just been liberated, Operation Dragoon (the Allied landing in Provence) was about to launch, and on the Eastern Front, the Soviet troops had liberated Minsk and were reaching the borders of Poland. Among the disarray, the disappearance of a pilot,

---

\* This (*découvrement*, in French, which is a neologism) is how the French lawyer, translator, and scholar André Chouraqui, in his translation of the Bible, rendered the word *apocalypse*, which is a transcription of the Greek *apocalypsis* and in the original doesn't actually mean "awe-inspiring catastrophe"; rather, it is the equivalent of the Hebrew word *gala*, meaning "to discover." In the Torah, it is often used to show that a secret or mystery has been revealed. This term, "uncovering," is used here to link the meanings of catastrophe, disappearance, and the revelation of a truth.

even if he was also a writer, was not seen as a crucially important event. The news wasn't published in the press until around August 9.

His fellow pilots held out hope for a while that he'd landed in Switzerland and been made prisoner. For many of his friends—even though the news didn't surprise them, for they had long anticipated this outcome, which Saint-Ex himself seemed to have accepted and perhaps even wished for—it took a long time to admit the reality of the situation. Tonio would reappear. Tonio the magician, so skilled at performing astonishing card tricks, who had survived so many accidents, who was like a rock, a death-dodger, a mischief-maker, he couldn't truly be dead. In the microcosm of Algiers, where the allegiances of the French were divided between Giraud and de Gaulle, the complete disappearance of probably the most famous and controversial aviator in the French Air Force led to fantastical and sometimes malicious rumors: Saint-Ex had landed and taken refuge in a monastery somewhere, he had been made prisoner, he had joined the Resistance, he had sold his plane to the Germans, he had been assassinated by the Gaullists. . . .

But these ravings ended when the country was liberated. Saint-Ex hadn't turned up, neither in a monastery, nor among the Vichyites in retreat, nor in a German stalag. It seems only his mother persisted for the rest of her life in believing, or at least in hoping, that Tonio was alive, hidden somewhere, having finally found inner peace while waiting for the peace of Christ. In 1945, a mass was held in his memory in the Strasbourg cathedral. In 1948, he was officially declared to have died for France, and in 1950 he received a posthumous unit citation.

As mentioned earlier, it wasn't until April 2004 that the rest of the Lightning was recovered in the waters off Marseilles, near the island of Riou, and formally identified. Until that time, several hypotheses were put forth.

One guess was that he was probably shot down above the Alps, and the debris from the plane was lying in an inaccessible crevasse somewhere. The most frequent suggestion was that he had gone down somewhere off the coast of Nice or Saint-Raphäel, perhaps even in the bay of Agay, the location of the château in which his sister Didi and her family had lived before it was destroyed by the Germans. Remember that during one of his first missions, Saint-Ex couldn't resist straying from his flight plan to fly over the property. Why not—knowing, as he did, that he was carrying out one of his last missions—break the rules one more time? In 1972, a posthumous eyewitness account came to light from a Luftwaffe pilot, Robert Heichele, who claimed that he had shot down a P-38 Lightning above Castellane in southern France while at the commands of his Focke-Wulf on July 31, 1944. This account might have matched up with the hypothesis of Saint-Ex's having made a little detour by way of Agay, but as Robert Heichele was himself shot down in August 1944, it was impossible to obtain any more details.

Already mentioned is the very late eyewitness account in 2008 from former pilot Horst Rippert, who claimed to have shot down Saint-Ex's P-38, declaring that he was profoundly sorry for having been responsible for the death of an aviator-writer whom he greatly admired. This story, although some did choose to take it seriously, is utterly implausible, and must have been a hoax or a ploy for media attention. Horst Rippert, who became a sports reporter for German television and died in 2013, was known for his mythomaniac tendencies. He was the brother of the singer Ivan Rebroff, with whom he had a contentious relationship; he thus waited until his brother's death to "confess" his wartime achievement, as though he had feared that his brother, who had a high media profile, would counter such a claim. Until then, Rippert had never mentioned this aerial victory, although he did boast loudly about the rest of his wartime exploits. Moreover, on his pilot's card, which kept a record of his wartime victories, nine enemy planes that he had shot down were noted—but none of them corresponded to the date of July 31, 1944. Why would he have waited more than sixty years to bask in the glory of this feat? Why, when Robert Heichele's account had been made public in 1972, did he not debunk it and claim responsibility himself? Let's also add that no official document, whether German or Allied, made note of any action on July 31 that led to the destruction of a P-38. What pilot who had shot down an enemy plane would not have informed his unit?

It seems that the only eyewitness account worthy of our attention is that of the German officer Erick Herot, who declared that he had seen an Allied plane crash into the sea near Marseilles on July 31, 1944. But we unfortunately have no precise details about this sighting, probably because at the time when it was reported, the hypothesis in vogue was that the Lightning had vanished somewhere near Nice. This scenario appears to be highly believable, however, for it coincides exactly with the location of the discovered wreckage, while when Herot delivered his testimony, no one was aware that there had been a crash near the island of Riou. Furthermore, according to Herot's account, the plane crashed without any outside intervention, which is consistent with the absence of any relevant after-action reports in the various military records. Finally, on the plane's debris (not that there was much of it), no trace of any impact was discovered.

Assuming this hypothesis is correct, one could posit that Saint-Ex, upon returning from his mission at an altitude where radar wasn't guaranteed to work (which explains why the Bastia air control didn't register his crossing over the coast), had plunged his plane into the waves. One question remains: how can this crash be explained if it wasn't caused by anything external?

From the moment of Saint-Ex's disappearance, the hypothesis of suicide has been put forward, so obvious was it that his morale was at an all-time low. As previously noted, many people were expecting this kind of ending: he repeatedly wrote about how the world seemed to have become inhuman and unbearable to him, and he declared often that death, which he had so many times narrowly escaped, mattered little to him—even that it was the normal exit for a fighter. In 1938 already, he had written, "Don't you understand that sacrificing oneself, risk, loyalty unto death, these are behaviors that have contributed greatly to establishing man's nobility?"[1] For Count Antoine de Saint-Exupéry, nobility wasn't a virtue: it was a requirement. And wasn't death in combat the ultimate sacrifice for a man of honor? In what was probably the beginning of 1944, he wrote to his beloved friend Silvia Hamilton-Reinhardt, "I am a pilot flying a P-38 in the Roosevelt Photogroup. High altitude and long-distance war missions. I hate myself too much to wish to return. I am far too uncomfortable in this decrepit shack of a body to feel very attached to this planet. . . . I have been insulted. So today I am quite content to be able to attest, by engaging my flesh down to its marrow, that I am pure. One can sign only with blood."[2]

But if "noblesse oblige[d]" him to fight and to risk his very skin, it didn't obligate him to die for the sake of dying. It obliged him only to serve, to be present, and to do his duty for those who were suffering. "I'm leaving for war. I can't bear to be far from those who are hungry. I'm not leaving to die. I'm leaving to suffer, so that I can share the experience of my family and friends," he wrote to his wife.[3]

Taking into account this acute sense of duty, though, it would seem that the hypothesis that Saint-Ex voluntarily tipped his plane into the ocean isn't plausible. He was in charge of a mission, and although he might have taken some liberties with regard to the specific objectives assigned to him, it seems practically unimaginable that he would have yielded to a personal and intimate impulse—in this instance, the desire to be finished with a life and a world with which he had become disenchanted—before carrying out his task. He hadn't forgotten the teachings of Daurat and the first rule of Aéropostale: the mail must be delivered, whatever the price. In *Night Flight*, he gave his character Rivière the "obscure sense of a duty greater than the duty to love," and beyond the love and hate of oneself and of others, one must sometimes accept death to be faithful to one's duty—but also sometimes refuse it. On July 31, Saint-Ex was charged with bringing back photographs, which he knew were important in the preparations for liberating his country. He knew they would save soldiers' lives and enable a faster victory at a lower cost. Hence, even if no factual element supports setting aside the hypothesis of voluntary death, it's hard to envision—with the heart—Saint-Ex allowing himself to succumb to weariness and giving up doing his duty.

On the other hand, we know that over the course of his career, Saint-Ex had many accidents, some of which were very serious and put his life in danger. On December 21, 1933, in the bay of Saint-Raphaël, he botched the landing of his seaplane; on December 30, 1935, during the long-distance race from Paris to Saigon, he struck a dune in the Libyan desert; on February 16, 1938, during the race from New York to Tierra del Fuego, his Simoun crashed into a gravel pit. Recalling his legendary distraction and his piloting errors is not to insult his memory—they were known to everyone. He hadn't changed at all in this regard in 1944, and as we saw, his apprenticeship and flights on the Lightning were peppered with numerous accidents, including the one that was serious enough to get the pilot grounded for nine months.

So, if he crashed "all by himself" off the coast of Marseille, it could be that he was the victim of a mechanical failure, especially since his P-38 had undergone some modifications not long before. Or perhaps his oxygen supply had run out, which would have been an "easy" death, for the aviator wouldn't have realized what was happening and would have passed out before dying. It's known that he needed a lot of oxygen, much more than normal. Maybe it was some other medical issue due to his general poor health exacerbated by his various excesses: after all, he had gone out and hadn't gotten much sleep the night before his last flight.

It's unlikely we'll ever know, but is it really that important? He took off for the heavens, and he didn't return; the symbolism here outweighs the reality. Remember: "So then the Lord Jesus, after he had spoken to them, was taken up into heaven" (Mark 16:19). The evangelist Mark, like Luke (24:51), reports that after his resurrection and after he showed himself to the apostles, Jesus was "taken up into heaven"—but only, he clarifies, "after he had spoken to them." This mention of speech brings us back to *The Little Prince*, where we're told that, before having met the little prince, the aviator didn't have "anyone he could really talk to." Another curious similarity: Major de Saint-Exupéry complained of the same thing at his base in Borgo on July 30, 1944, several hours before he was "taken up into heaven."[4] But hadn't he spoken through the voice of the little prince? Didn't the birth of the little prince act as a sort of resurrection for the exiled Saint-Ex, when he was at the end of his rope? And this "resurrected" person did speak—and after having spoken, he could take flight, for good.

IT'S A QUESTION OF words, then: the words of the little prince who wakes the sleeping aviator and, by the same token, releases him from a constraint, the prohibition from drawing and its consequence: the impossibility of speaking truly. What caused this extraordinary meeting was a breakdown: the plane's engine stopped working and the pilot had to land in the desert, a thousand miles from any sign of civilization. In a sense, he had been betrayed by the machine—by what was real—and ejected from the world that up until then had been his own, a world with people, noise, bustle, and grown-ups who spoke certainly, but without saying anything.

Something broke in his engine, then. Note that at this stage of the story, we aren't expected to know what kind of engine it is, never mind to assume it's that of a plane. The narrator had told us in passing in the previous chapter that, as he had not been allowed to become a painter, he had had to choose another vocation and that he had learned to fly planes; but when he is awoken by the little prince's voice after having fallen asleep on the sand, it is not immediately made clear how he ended up in the Sahara desert. We know that he's alone, without a mechanic or passengers, and that he risks dying of thirst if he doesn't repair his machine—but he could be in the same situation if his car had broken down. It's not until the next chapter that the information is provided to us: "And so, when he saw my airplane for the first time . . . he asked me, 'What's that thing?' 'That's not a thing. It flies. It's an airplane. It's my airplane.' And I was proud to let him know that I could fly. Then he cried out: 'What! You fell from the sky?'"[5]

Of course, the reader has anticipated this revelation, for he knows that the narrator had learned to fly and that the author of the book was himself a pilot. But it's odd, all the same, that Saint-Ex does not tell us from the start that he had "landed" in the middle of the desert because the engine of his "plane" had broken down. Instead he says, quite simply, "Something was broken in my engine," and suddenly he meets this funny little man he'll be able to "really talk to," since, at least for the time being, he's done with the grown-ups forcing him to talk "about bridge and golf and politics and neckties." In truth, it's mostly the little prince who will speak. The pilot barely speaks, other than a digression about asteroids and the costume of a Turkish astronomer in chapter four, and then about the size of the Earth, continuing with the part occupied by humans in chapters sixteen and seventeen. Mostly, he repeats the child's words, telling us the story of his travels, as well as of the last hours that they spend together at the end. The rest of the time he's content to question the little prince, often without getting answers, and for his part to answer the child's questions.

The aviator seems to take full advantage of the liberating request by which the little prince made himself heard: he draws, even commenting on and justifying his drawings afterward. It's true that his relationship with the little prince is formed thanks to his drawing of a sheep, and that their dialogue from then on centers around drawings—the baobabs (which for the child resemble cauliflower), the famous muzzle for the sheep, and its forgotten leather strap. It's that omitted drawing that causes the unrelievable—and perhaps unnecessary—anguish with which the story ends: "I forgot to add the leather strap on the muzzle that I drew for the little prince! He must never have been able to attach it to the sheep. So now, I keep wondering: what is happening on his planet? Perhaps the sheep has eaten the flower. . . ."[6] Even more than the little prince's death, which is a death only in appearance, it's this forgotten leather strap that lends the story its air of tragedy. "Look up at the sky. Ask yourself: 'Did the sheep eat the flower or not?' And you will see how everything changes. . . . And no grown-up will ever understand that this is truly important!"[7] How should we read this strange dialogue between Saint-Ex and himself? What meaning should we ascribe to this meeting that offered him the possibility of reuniting with himself, but that ultimately seems to remain unfinished, because it ends in anguish occasioned by an omission, something forgotten: a leather strap, an object that links two things together, allowing for attachment in every sense of the word?

So, before he was "taken up into heaven," the little prince spoke, and the aviator drew. The author, Saint-Ex, also spoke and draw in his book. He shaped the little prince's words and traced the aviator's drawings, splitting himself between the child and the man. But he also explored a reversal, or at least an unusual distribution, of the functions and abilities of children and adults. The little prince is a sage who teaches the aviator, and it's because of the permission he gives the aviator to draw that their meeting happens in the first place. In his notes on the text, Michel Autrand stresses, "The role of the child is to instruct the narrator. Indeed, he teaches him many things."[8] It's as though Saint-Exupéry had seized the opportunity that was offered to him—probably as a result of the drawings of the little man that he sketched almost obsessively—to write a tale for children. It was an opportunity to finally meet, or even better, to give life again, to "his" child: the child he had been but also the one he had never been, and thus it was an opportunity to be born again himself, in a way resuscitated. And while he was going through this very difficult period, doubtless the worst he had ever experienced, during the whole time of this birth* he was—according to Silvia Hamilton-Reinhardt and of all his friends—rejoicing.

THIS JUBILATION SHOULD NOT have been a surprise. *The Little Prince* was a departure from the rest of his oeuvre, but it was also, and probably above all, a departure from the rest of his life. The very birth of the character signifies a revolution—in the true sense of the word, a complete rotation—in Saint-Exupéry's relationship to himself up until that point. There was no child in his life. He himself was not a father, and it seems that he didn't suffer particularly for lack of a child; he never complained about his lineage dying out, and he never explicitly expressed a desire to procreate. In a letter to his mother dated from 1924, though, he did write, "I have a small, a very small desire to get married, but I don't know to whom. Yet I've acquired such a distaste for this perpetually temporary lifestyle! And then, I have great reserves of paternal love. I would like to have lots of little Antoines. . . ."[9] This desire to have "little Antoines," expressed in the conditional, didn't seem very pressing. In fact, during

---

* Let's note in passing that the writing—or better still, the production—of the book, from the summer of 1942 to the spring of 1943, took about nine months of work, the duration of a pregnancy.

his lifetime he made no concerted effort to fulfill it. Of course, he did end up satisfying his "very small desire" to get married by wedding Consuelo Suncin-Sandoval, but she was certainly the last person with whom it would have been sensible to have children.

The little prince, this "funny little man," was therefore the child conceived by Saint-Exupéry, the only son created from start to finish by an all-powerful father. In reality, he was a part of this father—a projection of him, in his very image—which is perhaps reminiscent of another Son. But the little prince, Saint-Exupéry's child, is also Saint-Exupéry as a child. With his little slightly round face and his halo of golden curls, he bears a shocking resemblance to the real little Antoine as we see him in family photos. Why go so far as to imagine, as Stacy de la Bruyère reports, that he might have been inspired to create the little man by a doll that sat imposingly in Silvia Reinhardt's apartment? Perhaps Mocha, her poodle, was the model for the sheep, and the boxer dog she bought for him might have become the tiger[10]—but, for the little prince, Saint-Ex had only to draw upon his own memories of looking at his reflection in the mirrors at Saint-Maurice-de-Rémens. The child that he created, this little prince who was also a little Antoine, finally recovered: couldn't he also come to represent a paternal figure, up until then lost in his archaic memory—a ghost with a hazy outline, like a threatening cloud?

Commenting on Jesus's famous speech, "Let the children come to me, do not hinder them; for to such belongs the kingdom of God" (Mark 10:14), French pediatrician and psychoanalyst Françoise Dolto wrote, "We must find our own source, that is to say, become our own father and our own mother and therefore our own child. . . . We have to invent ourselves."[11]

Saint-Ex invented himself in *The Little Prince*. The story is a face-to-face meeting between a child, who is a little bit sad, solitary, off-kilter, poetic, and sensitive, and a broken-down adult, who doesn't want to become a grown-up but thirsts for words of truth. Yet this meeting is mere appearance: the little prince and the aviator are indissociable from each other. They are one, Saint-Exupéry's recreated childhood, and both are the "source" that Françoise Dolto writes about.

Not incidentally, the only act that the child and the aviator undertake together is to set off in search of a spring so they don't die of thirst. And as soon as they decide to start walking at random, hoping to find a source of salvation, the very fact of leaving together for the same goal allows the aviator to return to his childhood for the first time, with the exception of the introductory chapter in which he tells us about the failure of his first drawings. Of course, one wonders whether the water they've gone in search of, walking side-by-side in the vastness of the desert, is just ordinary water that will satisfy only their bodily thirst. "'You're thirsty too, then?' I asked him. But he didn't respond to my question. He said, simply, 'Water can be good for the heart, too. . . .' I didn't understand his response, but I kept quiet. . . . I knew very well not to ask him questions."[12] When they finally discover the well at sunrise, it doesn't resemble other Saharan wells. It is like a village well in the middle of the desert, equipped with a pulley, a bucket, and a rope. The aviator hoists the bucket up to the surface so that the little prince can drink. And then, "'I'm thirsty for that water,' said the little prince, 'give me some to drink. . . .' And I understood what he had been looking for."[13]

This scene is reminiscent of another story of a well, with a thirsty man and water that had particular powers. "There came a woman of Samaria to draw water. Jesus said to her, 'Give me a drink.' . . . Jesus answered her, 'Everyone who drinks of this water will thirst again, but whoever drinks of the water that I shall give him will never thirst.' . . . The woman said to him, 'Sir, give me this water, that I may not thirst, nor come here to draw'" (John 4:7-15). Interpreters of the Bible agree in their understanding of this episode of the Gospel that Jesus, in exchange for the physical water that he asks the Samaritan to give him to quench his thirst, offers her spiritual water, which is not intended to satisfy bodily needs but rather a desire to accede to one's own truth.

This is just what the aviator understands: the little prince brings him water that, like baptismal water, allows him to be newly reborn. "I lifted the bucket up to his lips. He drank, his eyes closed. It was as sweet as a celebration. This water was something quite different than ordinary nourishment. It was born of the walk beneath the stars, the song of the pulley, the effort of my arms when I lifted it. It was good for the heart, like a gift."[14] It is because they walked together, taking the same path toward a source of life that was this well—which was not a simple hole dug at random in the sand but had been prepared for them ("'It's strange,' I said to the little prince, 'it's all ready.'"*), so they could quench their thirst—that the aviator and the child, his child, himself as a child, are able to share in this communion. And indeed, notice what the pilot remembers immediately after discovering the water that's "good for the heart, like a gift": "When I was a little boy, the Christmas tree lights, the

---

* And another Evangelical allusion: "Behold, I have made ready my dinner, my oxen and my fat calves are killed, and everything is ready; come to the marriage feast" (Matthew 22:4).

midnight mass and music, and the sweetness of the smiles were what made the Christmas present that I received so radiant."[15] And then, the well is discovered just as the little prince's star is again present in the sky: the star that points the way back to his childhood, and precisely to Christmastime, which celebrates the birth of a child—the child who will say, "He who believes in me shall never thirst" (John 6:35).

FOR THE SECOND TIME, then, the aviator returns to his childhood. It seems that he had already imagined this return with a surprising level of specificity. In a letter to his mother, written in 1940 as he was fighting against the German invasion, we find this sentence, which seems to have been retained in *The Little Prince*: "The only refreshing spring I find is in certain memories of childhood: the smell of the candles on Christmas night. It's the soul, today, that is quite desolate. We're dying of thirst."[16]

The curse had been lifted and he had rediscovered his source—the child he had been, who from then on could draw and speak. He had become one with himself and rediscovered the solace of childhood. The broken-down pilot, "even more isolated than a shipwreck victim in the middle of the ocean" who feared not knowing how to see sheep through their boxes and being "perhaps a little bit like the grown-ups," had finally heard and understood the essential message. "'Yes,' I said to the little prince, 'whether it's a house, the stars, or the desert, what makes them beautiful is invisible!' 'I am happy,' he said, 'that you agree with my fox.'"[17]

Now that they had drank together from the well, quenching their thirst, and now that the aviator had rediscovered the house from his childhood and the sweetness of Christmas evenings, the little prince had played his role. He could disappear and return to his rose, and that's precisely what he did right after. Saint-Ex had made him be born on an asteroid, alone and the child of no one. He had made him take a long journey, during which the little prince became convinced that grown-ups understand nothing, and that they lose themselves in their ridiculous and useless occupations. At the end of his journey of initiation, the little prince, after having awoken the aviator, gave him permission to return to his source, after parading out the ridiculous and the essential in life through his story, allowing the aviator to accede to the true wisdom and knowledge that only children hold—the original, primordial knowledge that comes from the heart.

"At that time Jesus declared, 'I thank thee, Father, Lord of heaven and earth, that thou hast hidden these things from the wise and understanding and revealed them to babes'" (Matthew 11:25). To attain this wisdom—this revelation—grown-ups must themselves make this journey, go to the desert to redis-cover their source, reunite with their childhoods: "Truly, I say to you, unless you turn and become like children, you will never enter the kingdom of Heaven" (Matthew 18:3).

Isn't this exactly what *The Little Prince* teaches us?

# 17

# THE ROSE AND THE SHEEP

Isn't it overstatement to summarize *The Little Prince* as, and to constrain it to, this sole lesson of the need to rediscover one's childhood in order to feel fulfilled and recover a sense of harmony in one's being? In part, yes, but that really is the essential lesson of the tale. The other philosophical or moral lessons either derive from it or support it, are secondary.

Hence, the famous statement "One can see well only with the heart. What is essential is invisible to the eye," the secret that the fox gives the little prince, is understandable only once it is possible to identify with a child who has the capacity to grasp the essence of things because he hasn't yet muzzled his emotions. And this is exactly what happens in the story: it is immediately after he has been able to talk about his childhood for the first time—about the house that hid a treasure—that the aviator suddenly understands that what makes things beautiful, whether the house, the stars, or the desert, is invisible. The little prince is delighted, then, that he finally agrees with the fox.

Likewise, the repeated criticism and the mockery of those grown-ups who never understand anything by themselves, who are bizarre and strange, who have forgotten things that are true, and who are represented by a businessman, an obsessive geographer, and a vain man, are intended to demonstrate that they are not like children, who know immediately and spontaneously how to perceive what is beautiful and true, and how to discern what is important from what is futile. They're not the ones who attach importance to numbers, count and recount the stars instead of allowing themselves to be moved by their light, and need to see large stones in order to assure themselves that mountains exist: "(We children) understand life, we have no need for figures!"[1]

The majority of the characters encountered in the little prince's journey support this idea of grown-ups. In truth, these characters aren't interesting in themselves; there's nothing to them other than their shortcomings, and any other grown-up could replace them. The king could easily be a general, the businessman a diamond merchant, or the geographer a butterfly collector. In addition, their order of appearance seems arbitrary: to invert them would change nothing in the meaning of the story, and the loss of one or the other wouldn't even be terribly significant. As Michel Autrand notes, "Besides their unexpectedness, these very conventional puppet figures are valuable only because of their colorfulness."[2] All the same, the character of the drinker leaves the reader perplexed, as it does the little prince.[3] If the other grown-ups illustrate ironically the faults that the narrator wishes to avoid—useless occupations, a sterile seriousness, and blindness to beauty—the drinker appears to be a man imprisoned by a dismal addiction, and we're left feeling not quite sure how evoking him fits into the tale. Meeting him certainly adds to the little prince's melancholy, but the lesson that we can take from the encounter, which is that it's awful to fall into alcoholism, seems out of place in the story's dynamic.

The same cannot be said for the animals. Some of them are only mentioned, such as the elephants that can eat the baobab trees and be eaten by boa constrictors, the boa that swallowed an elephant, the tiger that could threaten the rose (just like the caterpillars, except those turn into butterflies), and the migratory birds that allowed the little prince to escape. One is virtual in a way: the sheep, which is only a drawing and which even disappeared into a box, a little like Schrödinger's cat, becoming a sort of concept that has a very important function nonetheless, as has already been described. But two other animals play a role that is just as essential: the fox and the snake.

THE FOX APPEARS AS the little prince is lying in the grass and crying—he has even lost his gold scarf—because he has just come to understand that his flower is only an ordinary rose, his volcanoes are quite small, and he himself is nothing but a very little prince. Oddly enough, the fox proves himself to be the little prince's double, for he makes his appearance identically to the way the little prince does with the aviator: his voice is heard before he is seen. "'Hello,' said the fox. 'Hello,' the little prince responded politely, turning around but not seeing anything. 'I am here,' said the voice, 'beneath the apple tree. . .'"[4] The fact that the fox plays the same role for the little prince as the little prince does for the aviator is not unimportant. Michel Autrand notes, "He learns as much as he teaches, and, like the narrator, he becomes attached to the child. In sum, he takes on the role of the narrator as the narrator disappears from the story."[5] This very pertinent remark underscores that the little prince, the aviator-narrator, and the fox form a trinity. These three distinct people in the story are all part of the same essential being, a man searching for his unity: Saint-Exupéry. It is a trinity that cannot help but remind us of another trinity.

Moreover, a fox—an animal associated with flattery, lies, malice, and cunning—is a strange choice for one who delivers a message of truth and seeks to cultivate the friendship of the little prince, who up until then hadn't met anyone on Earth except a snake and some roses. It seems the fox was cast against type. Why did the author make this choice? Perhaps to make it understood that the fox cannot be reduced to what one believes he is, for behind his persona of chicken-devourer and cheese-stealer (in the fable by La Fontaine), he is wise and asks only to be tamed. Again, we must—as he himself will tell us—know how to see with the heart. Let's note in passing that when the fox delivers his message, thus passing on his knowledge, he's standing beneath a tree, and more specifically, an apple tree—a tree generally associated with the tree of knowledge, which was planted in the middle of the garden of Eden and bore the forbidden fruit. In any event, this animal makes us smile with his ambivalent attitude toward men, who hunt him but who also raise chickens; he moves us with his desire to be tamed; he enchants us with his poetic vision of wheat fields, which, just like the little prince's hair, are the color of gold and rustle in the wind; and, by his insistence on a fixed schedule that must be respected, he makes us think that perhaps Saint-Ex was mocking himself, as someone who solicited his friends' attention at all hours of the day and night. Above all, this fox delivers a double message of wisdom: that what is essential is invisible to the eye, and that one remains forever responsible for what one has tamed. It is this double lesson that the little prince will pass on to the aviator. The fox is thus an elder, like a father, who teaches. But he is also the child, who sees with the heart but who must be tamed, just as the little prince is for the aviator and just as the aviator is for those listening to his story. These three characters appear interlinked in this way like Russian dolls.

The snake, the "coil that was the color of the moon," welcomes the little prince to Earth. Like a zealous tour guide, he provides him with information about the planet; he inquires politely as to what has brought him to the middle of the desert; he evokes a philosophical idea by speaking of the solitude of men; but the important thing is that he offers his services so that the little prince, if he misses his planet too much, can return without incident. We know that he will keep to his word efficiently and tactfully.

A snake as the first to speak to someone who has fallen from the sky to Earth, a snake that will bring about death . . . It may be pure coincidence, but, if so, that would be the real surprise. How can we not evoke poor Adam and Eve, who similarly were placed on earth and, while familiarizing themselves with it, met a snake as their first interlocutor—a snake that, unlike the one encountered by the little prince, would reveal himself to be Machiavellian and deceitful? That was how Adam and Eve's snake would provoke the death of those who had listened to him, but unlike for his distant descendant in *The Little Prince*, his action was in no way one of compassion. In a way, like the fox, the little prince's snake was cast against type. After his initial infamy, this reptile has been looked upon rather badly. The Eternal himself announced his punishment: "Because you have done this, cursed are you above all cattle, and above all wild animals; upon your belly you shall go, and dust you shall eat all the days of your life. I will put enmity between you and the woman, and between your seed and her seed; he shall bruise your head, and you shall bruise his heel" (Genesis 3:14-15). It's no surprise that snakes tend to elicit such disgust and fear. And yet the moon-colored coil is presented in a rather sympathetic light: he is attentive, thoughtful, and ready to be of service. Certainly, he brings about death, at least in appearance, but he does it in the manner of a compassionate doctor who wants to alleviate the suffering of a patient with a terminal illness, and at the very request of the one who wants to leave. It frightens and pains only the aviator, who hasn't yet fully grasped the situation.

Indeed, on further reflection, if the first snake hadn't caused Adam and Eve to be banished from Eden, thus condemning them to death, they would have lived forever; that was the original plan. If this were true, they wouldn't have been forced to have children in order to keep humanity alive. Children exist because parents will someday die. From this, it would seem that the accursed first snake had, like Janus, a double face: he brought about death, and in so doing, he made it so that children would be born. Similarly, the kind reptile in the tale, by seeming to bring about the little prince's death on this Earth so that in reality he could return to his planet—lost in a sea of stars that henceforth would know how to laugh—allowed the aviator to have caused the rebirth—or birth—of the child he himself was. The little prince could then return to being a mere fantasy that had been necessary for the aviator to reinvent himself as a unified and harmonious being.

THE STORY, OR AT any rate this fairy tale, could or should have stopped there, with a happy ending. The aviator has been fixed, just like his plane, and the little prince has returned to his star, which is one among millions of others, all of which have become "a bunch of little bells that know how to laugh" and can console the pilot for the departure of his "little man." And since

Saint-Exupéry "rejoiced" while writing the tale and seemed to have come out from under his black cloud of depression, one might have hoped that he was going to find peace again.

However, the aviator himself—or his double telling this story six years later—didn't find the serenity that might have been his. In a sort of postscript, he writes, "Don't leave me so sad: write me quickly and tell me he has returned,"[6] which echoes the renewed state of despondency and weariness that Saint-Exupéry experienced after the book's publication. In probably the last letter he wrote, to Pierre Dalloz on July 30, 1944, the eve of his death, he closed with these words: "If I am shot down, I will regret absolutely nothing. The termite mound of the future terrifies me, and I hate the robotic righteousness of men. I myself was made to be a gardener."[7]

It is to the rose and the sheep that we owe the tale's depressing postscript: "So I wonder, what has happened on his planet? Perhaps the sheep has eaten the flower. . . ."[8]

IT ALL BEGINS WITH the little prince's request to draw a sheep. Of course, as one might expect with a fairy tale, the drawing will become a real sheep as soon as the little man has returned to his planet, so he worries about whether or not a sheep needs a lot of grass—a legitimate worry, given that his planet is "quite small." Then, although he's happy to learn that sheep eat shrubs and will therefore eat the little baobabs that pose such a threat to small planets, he worries about the fact that they also eat flowers, meaning that the rose he is so attached to is in risk of being devoured despite its thorns. One may wonder then why on earth the little prince wanted a sheep. Had he asked for a cat, for example, it would have been simpler: cats don't eat flowers, and what's more, thanks to Shrödinger, they're quite used to being locked up in a box, which is useful for transporting them from place to place. But a sheep is what the little prince wanted, and not just any sheep—not a ram with horns, not a sick sheep, and not one that's too old. Fortunately, the one he sees inside the box that the aviator draws for him is suitable.

The choice of a sheep cannot be insignificant, as we've indicated previously. Saint-Exupéry, who had to attend countless church services during his childhood and adolescence in the Saint-Maurice-de-Rémens château and at the Catholic schools he went to, must have been perfectly familiar with the sheep's powerful symbolism in religion. The sheep is omnipresent in the Bible, a sacrificial animal *par excellence* that for Christians symbolizes Christ himself. Tonio had surely heard this acclamation spoken just before communion during Mass hundreds, if not thousands, of times:

*Agnus Dei, qui tollis peccata mundi, miserere nobis;*
*Agnus Dei, qui tollis peccata mundi, miserere nobis;*
*Agnus Dei, qui tollis peccata mundi, dona nobis pacem.*\*

What's more, sheep were watched over by shepherds—a common profession in Biblical times—and it wasn't unusual for them to hear voices, as would be the case later for a certain shepherd destined for a glorious life that was nonetheless tragically cut short.

The little prince doesn't explain what led him to choose such a deeply symbolic animal, nor does the author, nor do the

---

\* Lamb of God, who cleanses all the sins from the world, take pity on us; Lamb of God, who cleanses all the sins from the world, take pity on us; Lamb of God, who cleanses all the sins from the world, give us peace.

book's interpreters. Since it doesn't seem that the choice had to do with a particular aptitude for representation on the part of the sheep, given that the aviator has to settle for drawing the box, one could posit that it is a nod to the author's Catholic education as well as to the sheep's "utility" in replacing a child who is about to be sacrificed. But one might also imagine that, in a rather perverse way, it was chosen precisely because of its ability to eat roses, which would allow the little prince to be permanently freed of his own rose—though it's true that a goat would have done the trick just as well.

Ah, the rose, about which there has been so much commentary and analysis!

The queen of flowers is loaded with—we might well be tempted to say buried under—symbolism. It is associated with Aphrodite; the favorite flower of poets; the symbol of Israel in the Song of Solomon; the emblem of the Virgin Mary; a rallying sign for countless secret societies; an offering to express one's ardor. . . . It would be impossible to list all the symbolic meanings for a rose. The little prince's rose in particular has provoked endless commentary, and there is no essay about the tale that doesn't mention it (including, of course, this one). All the same, these commentaries—which it serves no purpose to list or discuss here—are often somewhat esoteric, even convoluted, and in our view, they give this prestigious representative of the rosaceae family an exaggerated importance in the story.

To put it simply, the little prince and the rose are in love. She, a flower, acts like a woman, while he, a boy, acts like an adult.[9] But although this rose is of course very beautiful—it would be dismaying if she weren't, after she had made such an effort—she is also completely unbearable, capricious, vain, a liar, touchy, and sickly, to the point where the little prince, who was understandably fed up, leaves his planet in order to escape her. He is then overcome with remorse, guilty about having realized that his rose was only an ordinary rose after having seen a whole bush of them on Earth. The fox doesn't help matters by suggesting that he is responsible for her. The little prince immediately thinks he's obliged to go back to her, although he betrays a lack of enthusiasm: "You know . . . my flower . . . I'm responsible for her! And she's so weak! And she's so naive. She has only four thorns, barely of use at all, to protect her against the world. . . ."[10] Clearly, his speech demonstrates compassion more than love.

Many of the text's commentators have seen this rose as Consuelo, Saint-Exupéry's part-time spouse. It's likely enough that she did, in fact, serve as its model. She herself bragged about it, which is rather baffling, given that the flower in the story is not particularly charming: like Consuelo, the rose is unbearable, a liar, temperamental, demanding, and in need of protection, pampering, and admiration—and she coughs, too, just like Consuelo, who suffered from chronic asthma. Further supporting this identification is the fact that Saint-Ex behaved with his wife just as his little hero does with his rose. As he repeated tirelessly, he felt responsible for his wife, who was powerless and fragile in his eyes—which goes to show that love is indeed blind. "All of a sudden, I feel tremendously responsible for her, like the captain of a ship,"[11] he wrote in 1942 while he was writing *The Little Prince*.

Others have seen this rose as an evocation of Marie, Saint-Ex's mother. We have already examined the extent to which her son vowed his passionate and unwavering affection for her. Following in the footsteps of Bruno Bettelheim and his book *The Uses of Enchantment*, in which he psychoanalyzes fairy tales, the German theologian and psychoanalyst Eugen Drewermann proposes a reading of *The Little Prince* in his book *Discovering the Royal Child Within* that includes a long explanation of how the rose is a representation of the mother: she is loved with an impossible love, which therefore must be escaped. This argument leans heavily on tactical support from the armored columns of the Freudian subconscious, which, of course, means incest. An Oedipal interpretation, among so many others, that is perfectly conventional but without surprise or interest. In his notes, Michel Autrand writes, "But isn't it enough to see the rose as portrayed in the text as a representing Saint-Exupéry's views on women, and even on others, in general?"[12] This interpretation already seems much more sensible, notably because it allows us to shed light on this flower's perverse function in reopening the aviator's wound just as the little prince is in the process of closing it.

This being the case, the love story between the little prince and the rose, which is the subject of so many digressions, presents us with a problem. All literary assessment aside, it appears to be artificially planted in the middle of a story to which it doesn't add very much. To be sure, like the snake and the fox, the rose is endowed with the gift of speech, and because of that it fits well into the symbolic world of fairy tales, where plants and animals behave entirely like humans. But while the snake and the fox bear messages that orient the little prince, and therefore the aviator, in his quest, the rose plays no role in his voyage, except for having persuaded the little prince that he needed to leave by exhausting him with her whims. She plays her part before the little prince's travels and tribulations, and she is nothing but the cause of his "escape," for despite "the good will of his love, [he] had quickly begun to doubt her. He had taken words that were not important seriously, and he had become very unhappy."¹³ She was a triggering factor, but many other plants, animals, or circumstances could have played this role, and she is in no way an active participant in this extraordinary adventure. The little prince and his rose seem to be living a simple transposition of what Saint-Exupéry lived, particularly with Consuelo, and more precisely in the painful period during which he was exiled in New York. This part of the tale seems to be an "insert," an intrusion of reality into the fantastic world in which the rest of the story takes place. It is as though Saint-Exupéry wasn't able to immerse himself completely in an oniric world. Of course, one could object that from the start the tale is constructed around a situation taken from real life: a mechanical breakdown in the desert. But it is precisely that breakdown—a metaphor for the social, spiritual, and emotional stalemate that the author was confronted with at this point in his life—that will allow the aviator to encounter his forgotten, or refused, child, and to engage in the work of reuniting and taming, as the fox demands. That is the essential meaning, the existential and ethical message of the tale. It has nothing to do with the rose, who doesn't bear any message. She does express, and certainly with a certain poetry, the real difficulties of love stories, of stories with women, and of stories with others in general, as Michel Autrand says. But the story with the rose has nothing to do with childhood. It's a story of man—and of woman; it's the story of Saint-Exupéry, who wasn't entirely able to put distance between himself and the demons of his real life.

But why not? This rose, despite her faults, does possess a certain charm, just like her likely model, Consuelo; and this love story, like all love stories, is quite moving. So why deprive ourselves of it? Of course, the rose is a part of *The Little Prince*, and it is out of the question to set it aside or extract it from the story, even if only symbolically. But nor is it forbidden to consider it from a certain distance, precisely in order not to follow the little prince and Saint-Ex in their blindness, which, indeed, runs somewhat counter to the story's essential lesson: one sees well only with the heart. That lesson is true, but only if one has truly rediscovered a child's heart, accepting a kind of apparent regression that challenges one's way of being, and therefore, a fortiori, one's way of living. The rose's presence and the little prince's inability to "break her spell" turn the tale, as well as Saint-Exupéry's real life, into an unfinished quest—much like his great opus, *Citadelle* (*The Wisdom of the Sands*). As Nelly de Vogüé said, "You're a little like Christ when you're writing your *Citadelle*."[14]

THE AVIATOR'S JOURNEY OF initiation ends with the little prince's departure. He has understood that he's allowed to draw, listen to the song of a well's pulley, and open his window to the night and contemplate stars that know how to laugh. He can, without feeling guilty or embarrassed, leave the businessmen, scholars, and holders of phony powers to their sad occupations, and he no longer needs to conceal from the grown-ups that he is five or six years old at heart. How then to understand the *acte manqué*, the subconscious failure, by which he forgot to add a leather strap to the sheep's muzzle, making it useless for preventing the sheep from eating the flower? The aviator had grasped what was at stake: "I no longer cared about my hammer, my bolt, thirst, or death. On a star, a planet, my planet, the Earth, there was a little prince to console. I took him into my arms. I cradled him. I said to him, 'The flower that you love is not in danger. . . . I'll draw a muzzle for you, for your sheep.'"[15] We've already termed this an *acte manqué*, or a "subconscious failure"; could it be that "deep

down," as psychoanalysts love to say, the aviator doesn't consider
the idea of the flower being devoured to be a tragedy? After all,
he too could be a little tired of the constant references to this rose
and of the heightened sensitivity shown by the little prince, who
becomes "white with anger" and "suddenly bursts into tears" the
moment he senses that the object of his love had been ques-
tioned—a love, it must be said, that is not without ambiguity.

Hence, when the little prince meets five thousand roses in
a single garden, all identical to his own, he tells himself: "She
would be quite vexed, he said to himself, if she saw this. . . .
she would cough violently and pretend to die in order to avoid
ridicule. And I'd be obliged to pretend to care for her, because
if I didn't, she would really let herself die, in order to humiliate
me too."[16] The rose's image takes a real hit here—she is narcis-
sistic, feigning, and manipulative. So do the little prince's feelings toward her: he would be "obliged to pretend," and this out
of fear of being "humiliated." We are very far from a portrait of
passionate love! The little prince gives in to patent blackmail
in order to keep his rose from having to confront the ridicu-
lousness of her pretensions, which would explain why he can't
stand someone else tarnishing the flower's image. That image
wouldn't survive the slightest stain. Then he would be forced
to see the rose as she is, to become aware of his own blindness
and stop self-deluding with phony passions in which he feels
obligated to imprison himself.

Yet, although he had brought to light the rose's manipula-
tions, and although at heart he was no longer duped, he would
nevertheless go back to her, under the pretext (but did he really
believe it?) that she was so weak and naive he had to protect
her. This kind of compulsion to act while denying an unpleas-
ant reality relates to the addictions that constrain people to be

the architects of their own unhappiness, even though, at a fundamental level, they are perfectly conscious of their own self-destructive conduct. That's the way it is for people suffering from failure neuroses, substance abusers, and alcoholics, among others. A propos, we've already touched on the little prince's meeting with the drinker, noting that this episode seems to be rather useless, without a real place in the story other than to add to the hero's melancholy. Indeed, it does not enrich the little prince's quest—but it does become meaningful with regard to the intrusion within the fairy tale of the reality that this sad love story seems to represent. Whether deliberately and consciously or not, the author uses the confrontation with this character to put the little prince's behavior with his rose into perspective, disclosing its addictive dimension: the drinker drinks to forget that he is ashamed of drinking, just as the little prince feels compelled to fly to the aid of his capricious flower in order to forget that he feels guilty about being so dependent on the whims of a rose that is, ultimately, quite common.

The narrator himself is unable to free himself of the same addiction. While the story of the aviator and the little prince ends with the latter's departure for his planet, the aviator feels the need to pursue it six years later. He is no longer in the tale; he has returned to his "real" life and to his friends, who were "very happy to see him alive." He is sad, certainly, but he was "a little consoled" by the fact that he never found the little prince's body and so he knows that he returned to his planet, and he "likes to listen to the stars at night." In short, he's grieving, but things aren't so bad. And then "something extraordinary happens": six years later, as he is telling this story for the first time, he realizes that he has forgotten the leather strap necessary to make the muzzle effective, and this discovery plunges him into an abyss of tortured questions about what has become of the flower and whether or not it was eaten by the sheep. Questions that are completely in vain, for the story is over and the little prince is now in another world—the world of dreams, fantasy, and fairy tales. His return, besides the fact that it would have no meaning, because it would be expected, is impossible. Just as water never passes under the same bridge twice, the same little prince can never fall into the same desert again, according to the laws of fairy tales. But the narrator's self-interrogation weighs upon him so heavily that he adds yet another postscript, which is clearly not a part of the story—it's all by itself on the last page and in a different typeface—imploring the reader to give him news, or rather "good news": that of the little prince's return, if by any chance the reader were to find him thanks to the drawing representing the exact location of his disappearance.

What meaning should we ascribe to this seemingly excessive concern? Is it really so fundamental, to the point where "nothing in the universe is the same if somewhere, we don't know where, a sheep that we don't know may or may not have eaten a rose"? It's hard to persuade ourselves that it is. After all, even if this flower were eaten, another like it would probably come in its place, starting "as a seed." But, returning to the little prince's request for a sheep: it's fair to wonder whether, deep down, he might not have wished that the animal would rid him of this capricious and demanding rose. To be sure, he would never admit it, and he probably wasn't even conscious of it himself; but his way of repeating that he needed to protect her seems a little suspect, as though he were trying a little too hard to convince us. Even more suspicious is that, after becoming angry with the aviator for saying that thorns were of no use and that the question was not terribly important anyway, the little prince is perfectly lucid when describes the risks the sheep might pose for his flower: "Flowers have been growing thorns for millions of years. Sheep have been eating flowers despite that for millions of years. . . . Is the war between sheep and flowers not important?"[17]

So why does he so insist on putting his flower in danger by bringing back a sheep? Returning to the sheep's symbolic function to "remove the sins of the world," might one suppose that its function is precisely to cleanse the world of sinful flowers?

The little prince is divided between his love and his weariness, between the rose and the sheep. The aviator is divided between the world of grown-ups—his plane, the engine that must be repaired—and the poetic stroll through childhood offered him by the little prince. Saint-Exupéry is divided between the real-world contradictions and burdens he must bear and the sense of escape of a return to childhood truth, finally rediscovered and reinvented. The tale is born of all of these divisions. It is itself divided between the wisdom delivered by the child and the chains of the aviator's lived history that still shackle him, preventing him from going to the end of the path he's on, where he would reunite with himself completely.

The aviator feels the need to torture himself about a leather strap and the possibility of the flower—a rose whose destiny is to live the life of a rose—being devoured. Similarly, Saint-Exupéry, after rejoicing while inventing a little prince who could unveil the wisdom of a childhood brought back to life, falls back into the torture of loves just as capricious as the rose, quarrels with vain men and comic-opera kings, lamplighters illuminating useless celebrations, soulless rituals, and drinks that fail to quench his thirst, and petty accountants who measure false

values. He falls back to Earth just like the little prince, to whom
the snake had said, "You fill me with pity, you who are so weak
on this granite Earth"—"granite Earth," like the black granite
of the stone on mountaintop, the immobile stone that might be
an impassive God, a dead God.

It seems that ultimately, the book didn't liberate Saint-
Exupéry. From then on, he allowed himself only snatches of
childhood among friends and comrades, who spoke truthfully
because they were risking their lives. With them, he could laugh
and sing in a big playground for big children, where winged
snakes of steel waited patiently, immobile, to take them farther
than a ship could. It would be the only possible consolation: "I
know very well that if I were to die, I would feel cared for. It
goes back to childhood. Someone comes in to kiss you, rock
you, and put you to sleep."[18]

## 18

# LEAVING EDEN

*"Therefore the Lord God sent him forth from the garden of Eden, to till the ground from which he was taken."*
—Genesis 3:23

WHEN I BEGAN WRITING this book, I knew of Antoine de Saint-Exupéry as an aviator who had disappeared during the war and who had also been a writer. I had a vague memory of having read *Southern Mail* and *Night Flight* as a teenager and *The Little Prince* as a child. At one point, as a young man who was as altruistic as he was naive, I became interested in politics. I heard that this pilot, hero though he was, had displayed a somewhat guilty tolerance toward Pétain and his regime, who in my family were lined up against the wall and executed about once a day (symbolically, of course). Nonetheless, I found him a rather sympathetic character. First of all, he had a good face, a bit dreamy and kind; also, he was an aviator, which many children dreamed of becoming—especially if, like me, they had spent a good part of their childhood in Le Bourget, next to what was then called the "airfield," where Saint-Exupéry had often come to fly and where my mother had seen Charles Lindbergh land on May 21, 1927. Of *The*

*Little Prince*, I remembered little other than the drawings: the elephant inside the boa, the baobabs choking a little planet, and a little man with a long scarf floating behind him, who seemed to be quite alone. None of this, I'll admit, went very far. Like everyone else, I would regularly come across references to this tale—the use of the name or the silhouette of little prince in charitable works or on food products was, and remains, frequent—without them awakening in me a resurgence of curiosity. As Umberto Eco said, "The main character has transformed into a 'fluctuating fictional entity,' a character with whom everyone is familiar without necessarily having encountered him by reading the original work."[1]

But one day, I met a woman who was passionate about *The Little Prince* and had been devoting her energy and knowledge to the book and its author for years. Over the course of long conversations in which she introduced me to a world previously unknown to me, the rather banal idea came to me, as someone who has devoted his professional life to exploring childhood, that the universal success of this "little" book surely had something to do with its author's childhood. And so I formulated the hypothesis that this "philosophical tale," as it was called, was the bearer of a message, a lesson perhaps, that spoke to everyone because, as a child, Saint-Exupéry had everything he needed in order to become self-fulfilled and embrace the world. Having as baggage only my patchy knowledge (or worse, ignorance), I threw myself—with a rather irresponsible recklessness—into a book project that couldn't fail to validate my hypothesis, or so I was convinced. My benevolent and intrepid editor was on board with the project. From that point on, I couldn't turn back. I had to take action, which is to say that I had to live my days and a good part of my nights with Saint-Exupéry and his enigmatic little man. But my hypothesis was to prove impossible to demonstrate, even erroneous.

Very quickly, I became convinced of two things, which a priori seemed very discouraging for my project. The first is that, as I've said, very little is known about Antoine de Saint-Exupéry's childhood, or at least his early childhood, which is precisely the time when a subject or self is formed psychologically. The second is that The Little Prince is neither a children's story nor a philosophical tale, although it does borrow its traditional structure from the fairy tale, and it is even less of a "metaphysical treatise," as some have called it.

ALL WE KNOW ABOUT Saint-Exupéry's early childhood is the setting—a castle, a dwelling that befit an aristocratic family—and several anecdotes about happy times in which some well-behaved children, with just enough in the way of mischief and minor misdeeds, for which they were punished indulgently, freely developed their precocious talents. It's as though we're standing before an old, slightly yellowed family photograph of motionless figures with slightly blurred outlines, gathered in front of the camera's lens to convince us of their happiness. Time passes, punctuated with games and laughter, discoveries of treasure in the attic, and childish quarrels that are quickly forgotten—a time of reassuring, slightly outdated rituals, soothing adult benevolence, and a mother's unconditional love. No drama, no anguish, no pain, no real grief. War and François's death would come later, but by then childhood had already passed. Yet, someone is missing in the photo, and even the empty space he left behind has been erased. And behind the scene in this little theater, where a pleasant, enlightening, and agreeable show is taking place, looms the backstage, deserted and dark, populated only by unsettling shadows wandering endlessly in search of rest.

For Antoine, it is the meeting with the little prince that deconstructs the set, tears away the safety curtain, and sheds light on what is backstage. The book is an unveiling. The tale isn't a true fairy tale intended to entertain or strike fear; nor is it a philosophical tale, whose purpose is to instruct. Instead, it is a prayer that doesn't call itself by that name, perhaps because it doesn't know itself to be one. It is the prayer of a solitary child who couldn't grow up—that is to say, become fulfilled; a child who suffered from being exiled in the world of grown-ups, trapped in a grown-up body that he inhabited fraudulently, burrowing in when he would have preferred to live. "As I'm rather on the sidelines, I never told the grown-ups that I wasn't like them. I hid from them the fact that I've always been five or six years old at heart."[2] Thus, by his own admission, Saint-Exupéry stopped growing up when he was five or six years old—more or less the time when his father passed away and he became aware of it.

Louis-Ferdinand Céline, a writer who was Saint-Exupéry's contemporary and, like him, a heroic soldier (although in World War I), quoted a "Song of the Swiss Guards" from 1793 in the preface to one of his works, although it was likely made up:

*Our life is a voyage*
*Through Winter and through the Night,*
*We seek our passage*
*In the Sky where nothing shines bright.*[3]

In a letter to his mother dated January 1930, Saint-Ex wrote, "Now I'm writing a book about night flights. But in a more intimate sense, it's a book about the night. (I've only ever lived after 9:00 p.m.)"[4] And immediately afterward he evoked his nights as a child: "So then the day was finished for us, and in our child-sized beds, we were launched toward another day. Mother, you would lean over us, over this departure of angels, and, so the voyage would be more peaceful, so nothing would disturb our dreams, you would straighten the sheets, smoothing out any shadows or swells. . . . For one calms a bed like a divine finger calming the sea."[5]

For Saint-Ex, unlike for Céline, night was reassuring. That's how he spoke of it in *Night Flight*, and years later it preserves this soothing quality: "At night, reason sleeps, and things simply are. . . . Man puts his pieces back together and becomes a calm tree again."[6] Night is associated with the wonderful world of childhood, when a loving mother's hand could bring you closer to her. Night is a waiting Eden: "Rivière thinks of the treasures buried deep in the night, as though in wonderful seas. There are nighttime apple trees, awaiting the day with all their flowers, flowers that are not yet of any use. The night is rich, full of perfume, sleeping lambs, and flowers that don't yet have any color."[7] Note that the image of the garden, with its flowers and its trees, is everywhere in Saint-Exupéry's writing—he who, let's recall, ended the last letter he ever wrote by confiding that he would have liked to be a gardener. And in a letter dated May 1944, addressed to Madame François de Rose,[8] he speaks of the garden as a paradise of serenity and abundance, where everything comes easily without one striving to obtain it, just like before the Fall in the time of Eden where there was no need for suffering and sweat to be satisfied (Genesis 3:17-19). "In the gardens, one can walk. One can be quiet and breathe. One feels at ease. And happy surprises simply arise in front of you. There is no need to search for anything."[9]

But this paradise, this original place of innocence, precedes the fall, as we know from Genesis: "Fabien wanders in the splendor of a sea of clouds. The night below him is eternity. He had become lost among the constellations that he alone inhabits. . . . He walks desperately from one star to another, holding the useless treasure that he must deliver."[10] Fabien, the pilot in *Night Flight*, lost and alone, walking desperately from one star to another, foreshadows the little prince; and the treasure that he must deliver as he leaves the nocturnal Eden is his own life. As Michel Autrand wrote, "The death that the hero chooses is that of an adult who has reached the end of the night."[11]

In Genesis, we're told that the first humans were banished from Eden because they wanted to become the equals of their Creator by gaining knowledge, thus eliminating any divide between him and themselves. They became mortal because of it, and in order for humanity to continue after their death, they needed to have children. Sin, death, child: this is the progression that explains man's tragic destiny. Saint-Exupéry didn't want to leave this Eden. If one were allowed to stay there, it would be because sin didn't exist, and if sin didn't exist, then death would no longer be a necessary condition for life or for birth. Fathers wouldn't have to die so their sons could live. But in his own life, since his father had been erased (and his sin along with him), why should he be forced to leave behind this paradise, with its perfumes, its flowers, its apple trees, and its lambs sleeping through the peaceful night, just to wander, with death as his horizon? However, by clinging to this paradise-like childhood, staying in the soothing night, he makes it into a strange, dreamlike place, foreign to the reality of his life. Paradoxically, by wanting to maintain eternal childhood, he deprives himself of it; he cannot interiorize it as a memory—a part of his psyche—which would allow him to put it behind him. And it seems that he persisted in this fruitless battle, which he thought he could overcome by writing a definitive spiritual summa that would deliver the ultimate meaning of life. This was his great opus, which he worked on tirelessly throughout his days, *The Wisdom of the Sands*, about a son's inheritance from his father, which he knew he would never finish. Michel Quesnel wrote, "A passion for writing that is also a form of spiritual ascension. Saint-Exupéry pursued what only death could bring an end to, for want of a sense of completion: his posthumous book."[12]

In this context, *The Little Prince* begins to look like an "illumination"—a way out of the night. He was asked to write for children, so he created a child, his own child. He allowed himself to give birth, thus becoming a father. But his child was also himself. It was the part of him that was his own childhood, which he removed from its enclosure, its oniric prison, allowing it to live and speak, putting it face-to-face with himself: "He needed to build his own footbridge over the abyss and rejoin the other part of himself, across space and time."[13] He situated this very late encounter in a Biblical context, most likely without having consciously intended to; this is precisely what I've wanted to bring to light. The little prince says (and there can be no doubt that these are his most famous words), "One can see well only with the heart. What is essential is invisible to the eye." These words are remarkably similar to a verse from the Gospel of John: "He has blinded their eyes and hardened their heart, lest they should see with their eyes and perceive with their heart, and turn for me to heal them" (John 12:40). Is that a coincidence?

And what was invisible to Saint-Exupéry's eyes, if not his father?

The little prince, who was both a son and the son of a king, came to ask for a sheep: the sheep that would "take away the sins of the world," referring to the sins fathers had been committing since the beginning. He descends to Earth at the end of the night and awakens the sleeping aviator. Saint-Exupéry is reborn through the encounter with a child, who is himself—the child, son of the father—and so this child is the father of his rebirth. The line of descent is thus reestablished. By giving life to the little prince, Saint-Exupéry is able to rediscover little Tonio, who has a father somewhere in heaven. But henceforth, because Tonio left his sad little planet, he will be able to mention him and to pray, because the meaning of life cannot reveal itself without the father: "Pray then like this: Our Father who art in heaven, Hallowed be thy name. . . . But deliver us from evil" (Matthew 6:9–13). Just as with the other Son who arrived on Earth to provide comfort to men, the little prince may have seemed dead after he played his part and returned to the sky, but for centuries on end he would be there, alive. And Saint-Ex says to his little prince, "I won't leave you."

Sharp minds or fastidious exegetes may object that Christ had to be resurrected before he returned to the heavens. True, but the body of the resurrected Christ no longer exactly resembled that of living Jesus, to the point where Mary Magdalene didn't recognize him when he presented himself to her in front of the tomb. She had come to his grave and, realizing that it was empty and that the body of her Lord had disappeared, began to cry. The angels asked her, "'Woman, why are you weeping?' She said to them, 'Because they have taken away my Lord, and I do not know where they have laid him.' Saying this, she turned around and saw Jesus standing, but she did not know that it was Jesus" (John 20:13-14). Now—and here the coincidence is unsettling—Mary Magdalene believed she was looking at the gardener who took care of the grounds. "Jesus said to her, 'Woman, why are you weeping? Whom do you seek?' Supposing him to be the gardener, she said to him, 'Sir, if you have carried him away, tell me where you have laid him, and I will take him away.' Jesus said to her, 'Mary.' She turned and said to him in Hebrew, 'Rabboni!' (which means Teacher)" (John 20:15-16). A gardener: exactly what Saint-Ex confessed he'd wanted to be in his last written words. So who knows?

THE LITTLE PRINCE THUS seems more a parable than a fairy tale. This is not only because of its setting—the desert, the sky and its stars—and because of its words, which are reminiscent of the Gospels' *logia*—but also because of its teachings, which are delivered in the style of midrash. They aren't explicitly stated; you have go find them beneath the obvious narrative, which would be no more than a kind of palimpsest. The message is revealed when the aviator, having found the well with the child and drunk the water that is "good for the heart, like a gift," is able to return to his childhood, recreate it, and reappropriate it. After this episode, nothing happens that wasn't expected and announced: the little prince returns to his star with the help of the snake. As for the aviator, he has finished with his repairs, and the little prince explains to him that the story will end there: "I'm happy that you've found what you needed for your machine. You'll be able to go home. . . . And me too: today, I'm going home."[14] His mission thus accomplished, the little prince returns to his star and invites the pilot to return to his own life, since he's no longer broken-down. He found what his machine had lacked, he woke up, and he has repaired what was broken in his engine.

One might explain the meaning of the parable in this way: become your child again, find the source of your life, and recreate yourself as your own origin. Then, you'll see what's hidden—the elephants inside the boa constrictors—because you'll have put knowledge without soul in its proper place. You'll possess true understanding, the kind that comes from the heart—or, put another way, the kind that comes from the Spirit—with which all children have been endowed. They all possess this understanding, but sometimes when they've become grown-ups, they don't know how, or aren't able, or are afraid to express it. That is the universally relevant lesson that most likely explains the universal success of *The Little Prince*. Every reader receives it through its words and illustrations, even if he or she doesn't perceive it consciously.

This message is—to say the least—very close to that of the Gospels. We've examined their similarities, the places they overlap, the use of the same words; in some places, they're almost copies of each other. But beyond these specific instances, there is a sort of shared essential identity between these two sources of wisdom. While the Torah traces our origins back to an ancient couple, Adam and Eve, who will bear children without having been children themselves, the Gospels—which for the Christians extend the original union—tell us that God, the primordial Father and creator, incarnated himself in the child Jesus, and in doing so, refounded humanity and made the child the father to the man. And this child-God came to rid the world of sin and bring peace and reconciliation to mankind, between men and within them, just as the little prince gives birth to an aviator who has come to terms with his life.

So, might *The Little Prince* be the "Gospel" according to Saint-Exupéry?

# ACKNOWLEDGMENTS

I WOULD LIKE TO thank Delphine Lacroix. Meeting her was what gave me the idea for this book, and she helped me immensely with her knowledge, her wealth of notes, her attentive reading, and her advice.

Thank you to Jean Mouttapa, my editor, friend, and faithful guide.

Thank you to the Fathers of Chavagnes and to their Superior General, my friend Father Daniel, for their hospitality, which is always discreet, faithful, and generous.

# NOTES

## 1. The End of the Beginning

1. Virgil Tanase, *Saint-Exupéry* (Paris: Gallimard, 2013), 312. (For references to works not cited in a note, please see the bibliography at the end of the book.)
2. Antoine de Saint-Exupéry, "La paix ou la guerre?" in *Œuvres complètes*, vol. I, 357.
3. Syndicat National Des Pilotes de Ligne, eds. *Icare: Revue de l'aviation française*. No. 96, "Saint-Exupéry 1943–1944," vol. VI, Spring 1981.
4. Cf. Stacy de La Bruyère, *Saint-Exupéry* (Paris: Albin Michel, 1994), 440.
5. René Chambre, *Icare*, no. 96.
6. Antoine de Saint-Exupéry, letter never sent to Pierre Dalloz, dated July 30, 1944, the night before his disappearance, in *Œuvres complètes*, vol. II (Paris: Gallimard La Pléiade, 1994-1999).
7. Yvette Moiron, *Icare*, no. 96.
8. Cf. Antoine de Saint-Exupéry, letters to Pierre Chevrier, in *Œuvres complètes*, vol. II. Pierre Chevrier was the pseudonym of Nelly de Vogüé.
9. Jean Leleu, *Icare*, no. 96.
10. Antoine de Saint-Exupéry, *Pilote de guerre*, in *Œuvres complètes*, vol. II, 213.
11. There was also *Lettre à un otage*, which was intended to be the preface to a work by his friend Léon Werth, and which was published in June of 1943 in New York. It is comprised of six short chapters.
12. Stacy de La Bruyère, *Saint-Exupéry*, 409.
13. Antoine de Saint-Exupéry, *Pilote de guerre*, vol. II, 216.

## 2. A Strange Little Story

1. *Paris-soir*, May 14, 1935. Article republished in *Terre des hommes* in *Œuvres complètes*, vol. I, 372.

2. Cf. Stacy de La Bruyère, *Saint-Exupéry*, 414.

3. Eugen Drewermann, *L'essentiel est invisible* (Paris : Cerf 1992).

4. Cited by Alban Cerisier and Delphine Lacroix, *La Belle Histoire du "Petit Prince"* (Paris: Gallimard, 2013), 2.

## 3. An Enigma All the Same?

1. Antoine de Saint-Exupéry, *"Le Petit Prince,"* Reading Notes, (Brussels: Primento Éditions, 2011).

2. Eugen Drewermann, *L'essentiel est invisible.*

3. P. L. Travers (author of *Mary Poppins*), cited by Nathalie des Vallières, *Saint-Exupéry* (Paris: Gallimard Découvertes, 1998).

4. Title of a work by Jean-Philippe Ravoux.

5. Novel by George Sand that was published in 1849.

6. Novel by Anatole France that was published in 1918.

7. Novel by Frances Hodgson Burnett that was published in 1888, and then made into a film by Darryl F. Zanuck in 1939. The film was directed by Walter Lang and starred a young Shirley Temple.

8. Michel Autrand, "Notice sur *Le Petit Prince*," in *Œuvres complètes*, vol. II, 1348.

9. Autrand, "Notice sur *Le Petit Prince*," 1354.

## 4. A Planet Hardly Bigger Than a House

1. Simone de Saint-Exupéry, *Cinq enfants dans un parc*, (Paris: Gallimard 2013), 34.

2. Simone de Saint-Exupéry, *Cinq enfants dans un parc*, 39.

3. Alfred Thénoz, *Icare*, no. 69, "Saint-Exupéry 1900–1930," vol. I, Summer 1974, 78.

4. Antoine de Saint-Exupéry, *Pilote de guerre*, vol. II, 192.

5. Cited by Stacy de La Bruyère, *Saint-Exupéry*, 53.

6. Antoine de Saint-Exupéry, letters to his mother, in *Œuvres complètes*, vol. I, 724.

7. Antoine de Saint-Exupéry, letters to his mother, 778.

8. Simone de Saint-Exupéry, *Cinq enfants dans un parc*, 41

9. Stacy de La Bruyère, *Saint-Exupéry*, 47. It appears that Saint-Exupéry regularly underwent Bordet-Wassermann tests, used to detect syphilis.

10. Simone de Saint-Exupéry, *Cinq enfants dans un parc*, 33.

11. Antoine de Saint-Exupéry, *Le Petit Prince*, in *Œuvres complètes*, vol. II, 241.

12. Antoine de Saint-Exupéry, *Le Petit Prince*, 304.

13. Simone de Saint-Exupéry, *Cinq enfants dans un parc*, 34.

14. Stacy de La Bruyère, *Saint-Exupéry*, 48.

15. Antoine de Saint-Exupéry, *Pilote de guerre*, vol. II, 158.

## 5. From One Star to the Next

1. Antoine de Saint-Exupéry, letters to his mother, 1918, vol. I, 681.

2. Antoine de Saint-Exupéry, letters to his mother, June 30, 1919, 682.

3. Antoine de Saint-Exupéry, *Dessins* (Paris: Gallimard, 2008).

4. Cf. Stacy de La Bruyère, *Saint-Exupéry*, 90.

5. Bernard Lamotte, *Icare*, no. 69, 96.

6. Cited by Stacy de La Bruyère, *Saint-Exupéry*, 95.

7. Antoine de Saint-Exupéry, letters to his sister Monot, in *Œuvres complètes*, vol. I, 686.

8. Antoine de Saint-Exupéry, letters to his mother, 701–703.

9. Cited by Stacy de La Bruyère, *Saint-Exupéry*, 112.

10. Stacy de La Bruyère, *Saint-Exupéry*, 120.

11. Louise de Vilmorin, "Antoine de Saint-Exupéry," *Carrefour*, August 26, 1944.

12. Antoine de Saint-Exupéry, letter to his sister Marie-Madeleine, cited by Stacy de La Bruyère, *Saint-Exupéry*, 130.

13. Stacy de La Bruyère, *Saint-Exupéry*, 157.

14. Didier Daurat, *Icare*, no. 69.

15. Antoine de Saint-Exupéry, *Terre des hommes*, vol. I, 176.

16. "Sa philosophie ne fait pas le poids, estiment maintenant les philosophes. Et son pilotage n'avait rien de génial, jugent certains pilotes. Mais Saint-Exupéry est là." (Claude Yelnick, *Icare*, no. 69; "Philosophers now consider that his philosophy doesn't hold up. And some pilots don't think his piloting was all that great. But there Saint-Exupéry was.")

## 6. The Voice Crying in the Wilderness

1. Antoine de Saint-Exupéry, letters to his mother, vol. I, 764.

2. Antoine de Saint-Exupéry, letters to his sister Simone, in *Œuvres complètes*, 769.

3. Antoine de Saint-Exupéry, letters to his sister Gabrielle, or Didi, *Œuvres complètes*, 771.

4. Didier Daurat, *Icare*, no. 69, 140.

5. André Dubourdieu, *Icare*, no. 69, 155.

6. Antoine de Saint-Exupéry, *Terre des hommes*, vol. I, 191.

7. Antoine de Saint-Exupéry, *Terre des hommes*, 192.

8. Antoine de Saint-Exupéry, letters to his mother, 779–782.

9. Antoine de Saint-Exupéry, letters to Rinette, in *Œuvres complètes,* 819.

10. Antoine de Saint-Exupéry, letters to his mother, in *Œuvres complètes,*778.

11. Antoine de Saint-Exupéry, letters to his mother, in *Œuvres complètes,*783.

### 7. On Earth as in Heaven

1. Gilbert Vergès, *Icare*, no. 71, "Saint-Exupéry 1930-1936," vol. II, Winter 1974.

2. Georges Pélissier, *Les Cinq Visages de Saint-Exupéry* (Paris: Flammarion, 1951).

3. Antoine de Saint-Exupéry, letters to Henri Guillaumet, in *Œuvres complètes,* vol. II, 981.

4. Stacy de La Bruyère, *Saint-Exupéry*, 233.

5. Cf. Stacy de La Bruyère, *Saint-Exupéry*, 44.

6. Virgil Tanase, *Saint-Exupéry* (Paris: Gallimard, 2013), 241.

7. Cf. Virgil Tanase, *Saint-Exupéry*, 23 and 24.

8. Cf. Stacy de La Bruyère, *Saint-Exupéry*, 270.

9. Cited by Paule Bounin in *Œuvres complètes,* vol. II, 1461.

10. Simone de Saint-Exupéry, *Cinq enfants dans un parc*, 34.

11. Antoine de Saint-Exupéry, *Terre des hommes*, vol. I, 275.

12. Antoine de Saint-Exupéry, *Terre des hommes*, 783.

13. Antoine de Saint-Exupéry, letters to his mother, 724.

14. Antoine de Saint-Exupéry, *Le Petit Prince*, vol. II, 82.

15. Antoine de Saint-Exupéry, letters to his mother, vol. II, 82.

16. Virgil Tanase, *Saint-Exupéry*, 145.

17. Virgil Tanase, *Saint-Exupéry*, 145.

18. Frédéric d'Agay, foreword to Simone de Saint-Exupéry's *Cinq enfants dans un parc*, 9.

19. Antoine de Saint-Exupéry, *Lettres à l'inconnue* (Paris: Gallimard, 2008), 23.

20. Antoine de Saint-Exupéry, letters to his mother, *op. cit.*, vol. II, 848.

21. Stacy de La Bruyère, *Saint-Exupéry*, 317.

22. *Ibid,* 367.

23. Antoine de Saint-Exupéry, letters to his mother, vol. I, 702.

24. Antoine de Saint-Exupéry, letters to his mother, vol. II, 850.

25. Antoine de Saint-Exupéry, letter sent on January 3, 1936 from Cairo after an accident in the Libyan desert, letters to his mother in *Œuvres complètes,* vol. I, 784.

## 8. Tribulations

1. Cited by Curtis Cate, *Saint-Exupéry* (Paris: Grasset, 1973), 268.
2. Stacy de La Bruyère, *Saint-Exupéry*, 357.
3. Antoine de Saint-Exupéry, letters to Nelly de Vogüé, in *Œuvres complètes*, vol. I, 934.
4. Cited by Stacy de La Bruyère, *Saint-Exupéry*, 359.
5. Cited by Stacy de La Bruyère, *Saint-Exupéry*, 364.
6. The editor Viviane Hamy rediscovered the manuscript and published it in 1992.
7. Antoine de Saint-Exupéry, letters to Nelly de Vogüé, vol. II, 951.
8. Antoine de Saint-Exupéry, letters to Nelly de Vogüé, vol. II, 950.

## 9. The Beginning and the End

1. Curtis Cate, *Saint-Exupéry*, 312.
2. Cited by Curtis Cate, *Saint-Exupéry*, 327; Edward Weeks, "First Person Singular," *Atlantic Monthly*, April 1942. Accessed via ProQuest.
3. Antoine de Saint-Exupéry, letters to André Breton, in *Œuvres complètes*, vol. 2, 61–64.
4. Antoine de Saint-Exupéry, "La morale de la pente," in *Œuvres complètes*, vol. 2, 11.
5. Cf. Antoine de Saint-Exupéry, letters to Nelly de Vogüé, vol. II, 951.
6. Françoise Gerbod, "Notice sur 'La controverse avec Jacques Maritain,'" in *Œuvres complètes*, vol. II, 1244.
7. Jacques Maritain, *Pour la victoire*, December 19, 1942.
8. Françoise Gerbod, "Notice sur 'La controverse avec Jacques Maritain,'" in *Œuvres complètes*, vol. II, 1251–1253.
9. Antoine de Saint-Exupéry, letters to André Breton, in *Œuvres complètes*, 62.
10. Antoine de Saint-Exupéry, letters to Silvia Hamilton-Reinhardt, the end of 1942, in *Œuvres complètes*, 923.
11. Antoine de Saint-Exupéry, letter to Consuelo, cited by Virgil Tanase, *Saint-Exupéry*, 388.
12. Lewis Galantière, *Icare*, no. 84, "Saint-Exupéry 1941–1943," vol. V, Spring 1978, 51.
13. Antoine de Saint-Exupéry, *Pilote de guerre*, vol. II, 213.

## 10. *Et Verbum Caro Factum Est*

1. Antoine de Saint-Exupéry, letters to Nelly de Vogüé, vol. II, 944.
2. Antoine de Saint-Exupéry, "Carnet IV," in *Œuvres complètes*, 600.
3. Antoine de Saint-Exupéry, letters to Nelly de Vogüé, 944.

4. Antoine de Saint-Exupéry, letters to Nelly de Vogüé, 953.

5. Antoine de Saint-Exupéry, articles dedicated to Mermoz, in *Œuvres complètes*, vol. I, 338.

6. Antoine de Saint-Exupéry, articles dedicated to Mermoz, 934.

7. Antoine de Saint-Exupéry, *Pilote de guerre*, 180.

8. Antoine de Saint-Exupéry, letters to Nelly de Vogüé, 935.

9. Antoine de Saint-Exupéry, *Le Petit Prince*, 35.

10. Antoine de Saint-Exupéry, letters to Nelly de Vogüé, 961.

11. Antoine de Saint-Exupéry, *Citadelle*, 563.

12. Antoine de Saint-Exupéry, *Terre des hommes*, vol. I, 285.

13. Antoine de Saint-Exupéry, letters to Nelly de Vogüé, vol. II, 959.

14. Paul Claudel, *Contacts et circonstances*, in *Œuvres en prose*, (Paris: Gallimard La Pléiade, 1965), 1009.

15. Antoine de Saint-Exupéry, *Courrier Sud*, in *Œuvres complètes*, vol. I, 77.

16. Antoine de Saint-Exupéry, "Lettre au général X, in *Œuvres complètes*, vol. II, 330.

17. Antoine de Saint-Exupéry, *Citadelle*, 832.

18. Antoine de Saint-Exupéry, *Citadelle*, 726.

19. Antoine de Saint-Exupéry, *Citadelle*, 536.

20. Antoine de Saint-Exupéry, *Citadelle*, 632.

21. Antoine de Saint-Exupéry, *Citadelle*, 497.

22. Antoine de Saint-Exupéry, *Citadelle*, 726.

23. Interview with Dorothy Thompson, *New York Tribune*, June 7, 1940.

24. Antoine de Saint-Exupéry, *Citadelle*, letters to his mother, vol. I, 783.

25. Antoine de Saint-Exupéry, letters to Pierre Chevrier, vol. II, 972.

26. Antoine de Saint-Exupéry, *Pilote de guerre*, 213.

27. Antoine de Saint-Exupéry, *Citadelle*, 831.

## 11. Thou Art My Beloved Son

1. Cf. Pierre Lassus, *Être parents au risque de l'Évangile*, (Paris: Albin Michel, 1999) and *La Violence en heritage* (Paris: François Bourin, 2011).

2. Alain Vircondelet, *Antoine de Saint-Exupéry, histoires d'une vie* (Paris: Flammarion, 2012), 12.

3. Mikhail Alexandrovitch Bakounine (1814–1876), anarchy theorist.

4. Antoine de Saint-Exupéry, letters to his mother, vol. I, 780.

5. Antoine de Saint-Exupéry, *Pilote de guerre*, vol. II, 158.

6. Cf. Wolfgang Köhler, *Psychologie de la forme*, (Paris: Gallimard, 1964); Aron Gurwitsch, "Développement historique de la Gestalt-Psychologie," *Thalès* 2, 1935.

7.  Cf. Stacy de La Bruyère, *Saint-Exupéry*, 47.

8.  Stacy de La Bruyère, *Saint-Exupéry*, 47, note 5.

9.  Among the most well-known: Baudelaire, Flaubert, Daudet, Manet, Van Gogh, Gauguin, Toulouse-Lautrec, Lénine, Karen Blixen, etc.

10. Alain Vircondelet, *Antoine de Saint-Exupéry, histoires d'une vie*, 15.

11. Antoine de Saint-Exupéry, *Manon danseuse et autres textes inédits* (Paris: Gallimard, 2007)

12. Antoine de Saint-Exupéry, letters to Rinette, in *Œuvres complètes*, vol. I, 798.

13. Interview with Delphine Lacroix.

14. Antoine de Saint-Exupéry, *Courrier Sud*, vol. I, 52.

15. Antoine de Saint-Exupéry, *Le Petit Prince*, vol. II, 24.

## 12. Eli, Eli, Lema Sabachtani

1.  Antoine de Saint-Exupéry, *Citadelle*, vol. II, 409.

2.  Antoine de Saint-Exupéry, "Carnet III," in *Œuvres complètes*, vol. I, 559.

3.  Antoine de Saint-Exupéry, letters to Pierre Chevrier, vol. II, 954.

4.  Antoine de Saint-Exupéry, letters to Pierre Chevrier, 939.

5.  Cf. *supra*, 107.

6.  Antoine de Saint-Exupéry, *Citadelle*, vol. II, 537.

7.  Antoine de Saint-Exupéry, letters to Nelly de Vogüé, 949.

8.  Antoine de Saint-Exupéry, letters to Jules Roy, 336.

9.  Antoine de Saint-Exupéry, *Lettre à un otage*, 103.

10. Antoine de Saint-Exupéry, *Pilote de guerre*, 215. For context, it's curious to note that a form of this sentence is displayed, carved in marble, on a wall of the great hall of the Grand Orient of France, the largest Masonic organization in France, on Rue Cadet in Paris: "Si tu diffères de moi, mon frère, loin de me léser tu m'enrichis." ("If you are different than me, my brother, you do not hurt me at all, you enrich me") The quote doesn't match perfectly, most notably because of the addition of "my brother." There is no indication that Saint-Ex was a Freemason—in fact, it's highly unlikely that he was. The reference to Saint-Exupéry in such an important place for Freemasonry, when he was not himself one, highlights the universality of his message.

11. Antoine de Saint-Exupéry, letters to Nelly de Vogüé, 953.

12. Antoine de Saint-Exupéry, *Le Petit Prince*, 97.

13. Antoine de Saint-Exupéry, *Le Petit Prince*, 15.

14. Antoine de Saint-Exupéry, *Pilote de guerre*, 181.

15. Michel Quesnel, "Notice sur *Citadelle*," in *Œuvres complètes*, 1397.

16. Antoine de Saint-Exupéry, letters to Nelly de Vogüé, 951.

## 13. Draw Me a Sheep . . .

1. Cited by Alban Cérisier and Delphine Lacroix, *La Belle Histoire du "Petit Prince."*

2. Antoine de Saint-Exupéry, *Le Petit Prince*, in *Œuvres complètes*, vol. II, 237.

3. Antoine de Saint-Exupéry, *Le Petit Prince*, in *Œuvres complètes*, 302.

4. Antoine de Saint-Exupéry, *Terre des hommes*, in *Œuvres complètes*, 267.

5. Antoine de Saint-Exupéry, *Pilote de guerre*, in *Œuvres complètes*, vol. II, 216.

6. Antoine de Saint-Exupéry, letter to Pierre Dalloz dated July 30, 1944, not sent, found on his table after his disappearance, in *Œuvres complètes*, 1051.

## 14. The Annunciation

1. Cf. Pierre Lassus, *Être parents au risque de l'Évangile*.

2. Antoine de Saint-Exupéry, *Le Petit Prince*, 238.

3. Michel Autrand, "Notice sur *Le Petit Prince*," 1351.

4. Cf. Antoine de Saint-Exupéry, *Dessins*: winged person sitting on a cloud, 108; winged people in a letter to Léon Werth, 253; dedication to Silvia Hamilton, 255; winged people, 256, 257, 258, 271.

5. In Hebrew, Isaac (Is'hac) means "he will laugh."

6. Michel Autrand, "Notice sur *Le Petit Prince*," 1354.

## 15. The Ascension

1. Antoine de Saint-Exupéry, "Lettre au général X," in *Œuvres complètes*, 329.

2. Antoine de Saint-Exupéry, Letters to Nelly de Vogüé, in *Œuvres complètes*, 971.

3. Antoine de Saint-Exupéry, Letters to Nelly de Vogüé, 962.

4. Antoine de Saint-Exupéry, Letters to Nelly de Vogüé, 952.

5. Antoine de Saint-Exupéry, "Lettre au général X," 329.

6. Antoine de Saint-Exupéry, letter to George Pélissier, in *Œuvres complètes*, 1015.

7. Antoine de Saint-Exupéry, letter to Pierre Dalloz, in *Œuvres complètes*, 1051.

8.  Antoine de Saint-Exupéry, letter to Pierre Dalloz, 953.
9.  Antoine de Saint-Exupéry, letters to Nelly de Vogüé, 953.
10. Antoine de Saint-Exupéry, letters to Nelly de Vogüé, 965.
11. Antoine de Saint-Exupéry, letters to Nelly de Vogüé, 970.
12. Antoine de Saint-Exupéry, letters to Nelly de Vogüé, 971.
13. Antoine de Saint-Exupéry, letters to Curtice Hitchcock, in *Œuvres complètes*, vol. II, 985.
14. Antoine de Saint-Exupéry, letters to Curtice Hitchcock, in *Œuvres complètes*, 963.
15. Cf. Stacy de La Bruyère, *Saint-Exupéry*, 447.
16. Antoine de Saint-Exupéry, letters to his mother, vol. II, 848.
17. Cited by Stacy de La Bruyère, *Saint-Exupéry*, 449.
18. Antoine de Saint-Exupéry, *Lettres à l'inconnue*, 23.
19. Antoine de Saint-Exupéry, letters to his mother, 850.
20. Cf. Antoine de Saint-Exupéry, letters to Pierre Chevrier and Pierre Dalloz.

## 16. The Uncovering

1.  Antoine de Saint-Exupéry, articles on peace and war, in *Œuvres complètes*, vol. I, 357.
2.  Antoine de Saint-Exupéry, letters to Silvia Hamilton-Reinhardt, in *Œuvres complètes*, vol. II, 926.
3.  Antoine de Saint-Exupéry, letter to Consuelo, cited by Stacy de La Bruyère, *Saint-Exupéry*, 428.
4.  Antoine de Saint-Exupéry, letter to Pierre Dalloz, 34.
5.  Antoine de Saint-Exupéry, *Le Petit Prince*, 241.
6.  Antoine de Saint-Exupéry, *Le Petit Prince*, 317.
7.  Antoine de Saint-Exupéry, *Le Petit Prince*, 319.
8.  Michel Autrand, "Notice sur *Le Petit Prince*," 1351.
9.  Antoine de Saint-Exupéry, letters to his mother, 741.
10. Cf. Stacy de La Bruyère, *Saint-Exupéry*, 409.
11. Françoise Dolto, *L'Évangile au risque de la psychanalyse* (Paris: Points Seuil, 1977), vol. I, 43.
12. Françoise Dolto, *L'Évangile au risque de la psychanalyse*, 303.
13. Françoise Dolto, *L'Évangile au risque de la psychanalyse*, 306
14. Françoise Dolto, *L'Évangile au risque de la psychanalyse*, 307.
15. Antoine de Saint-Exupéry, *Le Petit Prince*, 307.
16. Antoine de Saint-Exupéry, letters to his mother, 849.
17. Antoine de Saint-Exupéry, *Le Petit Prince*, 304.

## 17. The Rose and the Sheep

1. Antoine de Saint-Exupéry, *Le Petit Prince*, 246.

2. Michel Autrand, "Notice sur *Le Petit Prince*," 1353.

3. "Et le petit prince s'en fut, perplexe." ("And the little prince went away perplexed," Antoine de Saint-Exupéry, *Le Petit Prince*, 271)

4. Antoine de Saint-Exupéry, *Le Petit Prince*, 292.

5. Michel Autrand, "Notice sur *Le Petit Prince*," 1353.

6. Antoine de Saint-Exupéry, *Le Petit Prince*, 321.

7. Antoine de Saint-Exupéry, letter to Pierre Dalloz, *ibid*, 1051.

8. Antoine de Saint-Exupéry, *Le Petit Prince*, 317.

9. Cf. Michel Autrand, "Notice sur *Le Petit Prince*," 1351.

10. Antoine de Saint-Exupéry, *Le Petit Prince*, 316.

11. Antoine de Saint-Exupéry, letters to Silvia Hamilton-Reinhardt, 924.

12. Michel Autrand, "Notice sur *Le Petit Prince*," 1352.

13. Antoine de Saint-Exupéry, *Le Petit Prince*, 259.

14. Letter from Nelly de Vogüé, cited by Stacy de La Bruyère, *Saint-Exupéry*, 446.

15. Antoine de Saint-Exupéry, *Le Petit Prince*, 256.

16. Antoine de Saint-Exupéry, *Le Petit Prince*, 290.

17. Antoine de Saint-Exupéry, *Le Petit Prince*, 254.

18. Antoine de Saint-Exupéry, letters to Pierre Chevrier, 974.

## 18. Leaving Eden

1. Umberto Eco, *Confessions d'un jeune romancier* (Paris: Grasset 2013), 114.

2. Variation on the manuscript of *The Little Prince* cited by Alban Cerisier and Delphine Lacroix, *La Belle Histoire du "Petit Prince,"* 2.

3. Louis-Ferdinand Céline, *Voyage au bout de la nuit*, (Paris: Denoël et Steele, 1932).

4. Antoine de Saint-Exupéry, letters to his mother, 781.

5. Antoine de Saint-Exupéry, letters to his mother, 781.

6. Antoine de Saint-Exupéry, *Pilote de guerre*, 119.

7. Antoine de Saint-Exupéry, *Vol de nuit*, in *Œuvres complètes*, vol. I, 157.

8. Yvonne de Rose, a friend of Saint-Ex's in New York.

9. Antoine de Saint-Exupéry, letter to Madame de Rose, in *Œuvres complètes*, vol. 2, 1048.

10. Antoine de Saint-Exupéry, letter to Madame de Rose, 158.

11. Michel Autrand, "Notice sur *Le Petit Prince*," 1354.

12. Michel Questel, "Notice sur *Citadelle*," 1396.

13. Antoine de Saint-Exupéry, *Citadelle*, 831.

14. Antoine de Saint-Exupéry, *Le Petit Prince*, 310.

# BIBLIOGRAPHY

Cate, Curtis. *Saint-Exupéry*. Paris: Grasset, 1973.

Cerisier, Alban, and Lacroix, Delphine. *La Belle Histoire du* Petit Prince. Paris: Gallimard, 2013.

Chevrier, Pierre. *Antoine de Saint-Exupéry*. Paris: Gallimard, 1949.

Drewermann, Eugen. *L'essentiel est invisible*. Paris: Cerf, 1992.

Dudan, Pierre. *Antoine et Robert*. Lausanne: Antagnes, 1981.

Forest, Philippe and Audeguy, Stéphane. *L'Enfance de la littérature*. Paris: Gallimard, 2013.

Guéno, Jean-Pierre. *La Mémoire du « Petit Prince »*. Paris: Jacob-Duvernet, 2009.

*Icare. Revue de l'aviation française*, no. 69 (1974), no. 71 (1974–1975), no. 75 (1975), no. 78 (1976), no. 84 (1978), no. 96 (1981).

La Bruyère, Stacy de. *Saint-Exupéry*. Paris: Albin Michel, 1994.

Lacroix, Delphine. *Saint-Exupéry, pilote de guerre*. Paris: Gallimard, 2013.

Monin, Emmanuel-Yves. *L'Ésotérisme du « Petit Prince »*. Paris: Dervy, 2012.

Pélissier, Georges. *Les Cinq Visages de Saint-Exupéry*. Paris: Flammarion, 1951.

Persane-Nastorg, Michèle. *Marie de Saint-Exupéry*. Paris: Triomphe, 2013.

Ravoux, Jean-Philippe. *Donner un sens à l'existence. Pourquoi « Le Petit Prince » est le plus grand traité de métaphysique du XXe siècle*. Paris: Robert Laffont, 2008.

Saint-Exupéry, Antoine de. *Œuvres complètes*, 2 vols. Paris: Gallimard La Pléiade, 1994–1999.

Saint-Exupéry, Antoine de. *Dessins*. Paris: Gallimard, 2008.

Saint-Exupéry, Antoine de. *Lettres à l'inconnue*. Paris: Gallimard, 2008.

Saint-Exupéry, Simone. *Cinq enfants dans un parc*. Paris: Gallimard, 2000.

Tanase, Virgil. *Saint-Exupéry*. Paris: Gallimard, 2013.

Vallières, Nathalie des. *Saint-Exupéry*. Paris: Gallimard Découvertes, 1998.

Vircondelet, Alain. *Antoine de Saint-Exupéry, histoires d'une vie*. Paris: Flammarion, 2012.

Werth, Léon. *Saint-Exupéry tel que je l'ai connu*. Paris: Viviane Hamy, 1994.